Advance Praise

for

Tremors

short fiction by California writers

❧

We should expect a few tremors from California and particularly from Pleasant Hill, where these writers gather.

Tremors do occur along fault lines under the surface there; and we may feel them just under surface of these short stories, too: tremors such as a first, forced kiss on the White Cliffs of Dover, becoming sweet; a sudden glimpse of a white hood, becoming a mirror, contrary to a self-image in Florida; devil dancers on Route 66; an expression of faith before an execution in Louisiana; a realization of faith before a natural death in a hospital; three wishes coming true in dire straits, so that an agreeable tom-cat turns into a comely Adonis (these tremors can be amusing, too).

There are a few full earthquakes: the destruction of a community during the Partition of India; the devastation of lives during drug wars in El Cerrito; pathos in an AIDS hospice in San Francisco. But most are tremors just under the surface in these stories.

This anthology lives up to its name; and it engages us beyond geographical boundaries as these authors draw from personal experiences far and wide: India, Europe, the East Coast, Deep South, Far West and the beaches of Hawaii. One piece of flash fiction, told through the eyes of an American boy in London, delivers its tremor with a rap on the boy's willing knuckles, a reminder about the virtue of mutual responsibility and companionship.

The anthology gives us engaging examples of flash fiction along with some examples of historical fiction, the latter with dialect. The writers draw from social depths, too, when characters so diverse as Joe DiMaggio, T-Bone, and Gandhi appear in the stories. The anthology is full of surprises, pleasant.

May we read more from these writers some day!

- Dr. S. A. Mousalimas, Oxford University, England

When a writer who truly loves to write puts pen to paper, the results can be a profound outpouring of creative expression that delights the senses. This group of dedicated writers has achieved this very goal. Their stories blend seamlessly to form a quilt of literary excellence that highlights their unique writing styles and mirrors their personal life experiences. While not a fan of short stories, I read these with awe at what can be achieved by those with creative talent. I feel honored to be among the first to be allowed the privilege of experiencing this very special gift to the reading public.

- Sharon H. Stewart, Editor

This collection of vibrant stories covers the spectrum of human experience, with ordinary people telling the stories of fascinating lives. Moving across culture, class, gender, race, and myriad life circumstances, the writers here employ humor and gravity to sketch out scenes as compelling as they are diverse.

- Riam Griswold, Book Reviewer

The authors of *Tremors* are called the "Saturday Word Painters" by their writing teacher Janice De Jesus. They have triumphantly lived up to that name, offering a collection as varied as the authors themselves. Their memorable stories are filled with childhood imaginings, the thrill of defying the law, surviving adolescence, the tragedy of racial conflict, the emotional price of war, and with loss, love and the solace of remembrance. Most notably, these eight authors have given hope to all those who work so hard to learn the craft of writing. They have proven it can most definitely be achieved, with tenacity and grace.

- Lyn Roberts, Literary Editor

tremors

short fiction
by California writers

Ken Branch   Douglas Burgess   Franklin T. Burroughs

Maya Mitra Das   Carlos de Jalisco   Sue Hummel

Cecilia Pugh   Lynne Grant-Westenhaver

Douglas Burgess (signature)

Azalea Art Press
Berkeley . California

ISBN: 978-0-9908456-0-7

CONTENTS

❧

Foreword by Janice De Jesus   *i*

Ken Branch   **1**
The Matchmakers' Italian Dinner   2
Ron Diamond (excerpts from a novel)   8

Maya Mitra Das   **41**
The House by the Creek   42
Manjari and the Ballad of Peace   51

Douglas Burgess   **75**
Standin' at the Crossroads   76
Bugle Calls   85
Army Brat Stories:
      Camaraderie   92
      The General   96
      The Pocket Knife   99
Long Shots   105

Sue Hummel   **109**
Alice and Margaret   110
After the Fight   121
Playing the President   123
Holding Hands   138

Franklin T. Burroughs   **143**
The Devil Dancers on Route 66   144

Cecilia Pugh   **181**
Cemetery Hill   182
From My Window   188
Table Number Fifty   195
Hog Maws, Chittlins 'n Pig's Feet   206
Waiting in Line   213

Carlos de Jalisco   **219**
Thrill Hill   220
Ice Breaker   224
Pavlov's Revenge   232
Night of the Dragon   237

Lynne Grant-Westenhaver   **257**
Saving Charlie   258
Two Weeks   283
A Beach Day: Big Island Hawaii   287

Acknowledgments   **289**
Contact   **294**

Foreword

❧

During a visit to Monterey, I came across a lovely anthology of fiction writers. It inspired me to see if the Creative Writing class I had been teaching might be interested in creating their own collection.

My students were more than enthusiastic. The more we talked about having an anthology to call our own, the more it stoked our literary fire. Submissions began pouring in. Eight souls braved the waters of writing, critiquing, revising, and editing their work as well as learning the business side from their publisher, Karen Mireau. Like a mother nurturing her children, I watched them blossom, grow and become more autonomous.

What I cherish most is that we became a family. We learned to appreciate each other's writing but also to trust and respect one other. I love this intimate group and I am so proud of the way these writers have navigated the challenges of their journey toward publication.

And so it is with immense joy that I present these authors to you. Their stories will amaze you, entertain you, inform you, and even enlighten you. They have truly embraced the philosophy of crafting and cultivating the fine art of creative fiction.

- Janice De Jesus
Creative Writing Instructor
Pleasant Hill Recreation and Park District

tremors

short fiction
by California writers

Ken Branch

Ken Branch is a native San Franciscan, whose family dates back to the Gold Rush of 1849. He attended Catholic parochial schools until he was liberated at Berkeley at the University of California where he graduated in 1960 with a major in Political Science.

Needing to find gainful occupation, he became a lawyer, specializing in real estate trial litigation. He has been married for fifty years to a long-suffering, beautiful woman, Cecilia Louise Branch. They have been blessed with two intellectually gifted sons and two wonderful grandchildren.

Ken has recently discovered the wonder of creative writing where he is, effectively, a kid in a candy store.

The Matchmakers' Italian Dinner

⚬

Sitting by the fireplace listening to my Aunt Kay's stories during the holidays is what I remember most fondly about my favorite aunt. When I was growing up, not only did Aunt Kay make the 1930s come alive with her animated accounts, but she introduced to me a love of baseball lore that remains with me to this day. And boy, did she have a story to tell!

Long before everyone knew him as the New York Yankee great Joe DiMaggio, he was Giuseppe Paolo DiMaggio, known to the minor league baseball team, the San Francisco Seals, as "Joe DiMag," pronounced in a semi-French way—as in *"dee-maj."* Earlier that summer, Joe had set the Pacific Coast League record for hitting safely in sixty-one straight League games. The Major Leagues was seriously looking at this homegrown, nineteen-year-old phenom whose face resembled a map of Italy—land of his parental origin.

Aunt Kay's story began when she was getting dressed for a dinner in mid-September 1933 to meet the would-be celebrity's family. Before the world knew him as a sports legend, an icon and one-time husband of Marilyn Monroe, Joe "DiMag" was blessed with Sicilian good looks accented with a boyish, gawky, gangly yet athletic form. That was the boy that my Aunt Kay dated when she was just an eighteen-year-old ingénue.

Back in the day, Aunt Kay was known as Kay Lucci, a Naples-born, southern Italian girl who grew up to be a rather cosmopolitan young lady. Their date was set up by Joe's cousin, Guido Lencioni, a seminarian working at Sacred Heart Catholic Church in mid-town San Francisco that summer. All Catholic seminarians, during the later stages of their vocational training, were assigned to assist at various parishes in their home diocese to get a flavor of a parish priest's life. Guido, notwithstanding his priestly vocation, had a southern Italian's eye for attractive young women. When Guido set his eyes on my Aunt Kay, one of the young parishioners, he knew he'd won the matchmakers' jackpot. He heard she was quick-witted, smart, a great dancer, and Italian to boot—everything that would garner his aunt, Mama Rosalia DiMaggio's approval.

Aunt Kay would tell me later that she hadn't known all those times she attended mass at Sacred Heart Church that, unbeknownst to her, she was a specimen closely scrutinized by none other than Joe DiMaggio's "priestly cousin."

"I know it's what your generation would now call 'creepy,' a young woman being observed by a priest-in-training during mass," Aunt Kay said. "But he was on a mission—to find a good match for his cousin."

Kay found out that Guido's family came from Nochera, where her Papa Frank Lucci's family also hailed from and based on that connection alone, a dinner invitation to the Lucci home was arranged, despite the

3

fact that Papa Frank was a classic Italian anti-clerical Socialist, who didn't quite favor the Catholic Church, to put it mildly. But Papa Frank ignored Guido's religious role in favor of accommodating his cousin, Joe DiMaggio's rising baseball star status.

Acting the role of the proper young lady, Kay remained poised during the dinner, allowing the men to orchestrate the whole dinner event, beginning with the conversation. Guido launched the conversational gambit that had the previous approval of his mother, Lucia, and Joe's parents, Mama Rosalia and Papa Giuseppe DiMaggio.

"My Mama and Aunt Rosalia are really upset with the girls who are throwing themselves at Joe," Guido said, as he helped himself to more *Pasta e Fagioli*, one of the most famous dishes of Naples. "They wait for him at the Seals' clubhouse door wearing dresses that leave very little to the imagination and try to finagle Joe into taking them out, which he sometimes does. This scares my Aunt Rosalia who would love nothing more than to see her beloved Joe settle down with a nice Italian girl."

Aunt Kay recalls the time she flinched when she heard those words come out of Guido's mouth. She looked over at her mother and *la chef della casa*, Carmela Lucci. Kay read her mother's expression clearly: the bait of a young, handsome, potentially wealthy and soon-to-be famous Italian American athlete was too hard to resist.

"Poor Mama DiMaggio, I cry for her," said Mama Lucci, clasping her hands together. "What can my family do to prevent such a tragedy from happening to your family?"

Guido folded his arms. "If only Joe were to meet one of your daughters. This could be an answer to my aunt's prayers."

Kay's gaze darted from her Mama to Guido and back to her mother again. She was beginning to feel a bit queasy and she knew it wasn't because of the food.

"My older daughter Maria is already spoken for and is a year older than your cousin, Joe," said Mama Carmela Lucci. "But my daughter, Caterina, is suitable and available. She may be the ideal choice."

The second Kay heard her mother utter her baptismal name, her heart sank. By evening's end, Guido had been commissioned by Mama Lucci to accommodate Mama Rosalia DiMaggio's wishes and set up a date for Kay with Joe. The matchmakers' deal had been sealed.

But, as far as Kay was concerned, her fate had not been decided. Joe, not knowing how to drive a car, "picked Kay up" at her home in San Francisco's Duboce district on foot on the following Saturday for their date. They walked to Market Street and caught a jitney to a decent downtown restaurant. An unsophisticated fisherman's son whose school attendance was spotty at best, Joe could only talk about himself, about fishing boats and baseball—always about baseball, a subject that Kay didn't give a damn about.

Then Kay thought it would be refreshing to show Joe her quick-witted self—that she wasn't just some good-mannered Italian girl willing to bow down to a man's whims. She cleared her throat as she smoothed the folds of her skirt.

"I intend to take typing lessons, go to college and make a name for myself and not just sit around home darning socks and memorizing pasta recipes," Kay told Joe, matching his gaze with hers. She was undaunted by his athletic masculinity as she tossed her wavy, dark brown hair. "What do you think about that?"

The expression on Joe's face, the way his jaw seemed to hang there, Kay remembers to this day, was priceless. She recalled beaming while giving herself a virtual pat on the back and chuckling on the inside.

When she got home, as expected, her sister, Maria cornered her for details about their date. Maria had always been competitive and even while she was engaged herself, Kay knew that deep inside, Maria secretly wished Kay wouldn't make as good a match as she had.

Hoping to provide her sister enough details, Kay launched her rapid-fire summary of the date.

"I was put off by his dating manners and not to mention, his ego. Plus, do you know what he had the nerve to wear on a date? White socks with black leather shoes, among other clothing disasters. White socks, I tell you!"

Then Kay brushed past her sister up the stairs toward her room, a smug smile on her face. Several years later, Kay told me that she had achieved a victorious coup that night. Indeed, she hadn't fallen victim to the great Joe DiMaggio's supposedly irresistible charms.

"But Aunt Kay," I remembered my ten-year-old self asking. "You turned down the great Joe DiMaggio. He could have been your husband."

The fact that I had an intense passion for baseball went unnoticed by my family.

"Joe DiMaggio could've been my uncle," I said, looking down as the dying embers of the fireplace settled on a cold, holiday night. "I would've been his nephew."

"My dear," said Aunt Kay, as she cupped my chin in her hands. "It doesn't matter who your uncle turned out to be. You are my nephew, and a very special nephew you are! You can be whomever you wish to be—even greater than the great Joe DiMaggio himself. I know that whatever you choose to do in life, you will be the greatest."

Years later, armed with my law degree, my passion for baseball still intact, I looked at my beautiful fiancée in front of me, at the cusp of exchanging our vows. One thing was for sure—Aunt Kay was right. I'd dated my share of interesting women, some celebrities, but true love had nothing to do with fame or fortune.

I turned to see the pride in my Aunt Kay's face as she sat in the church pew, dabbing her eyes with her handkerchief.

Ron Diamond

(excerpts from a novel)

◆

In order to fully participate as an adult male warrior in the tribe, Ron Diamond, the twelve-year-old grandson of the tribal chief or cacique, has to complete the coming-of-age rites. His coming-of-age day dawns. He is not allowed food, but only water. Stark naked and barefoot, he is given an empty bowl at the edge of the village and told to go and find his life.

Nightfall. He goes to a fire in the distance, thinking it's his grandfather on a hunt. No, it's just a fire. Approaching the fire, he hears words in an unknown language, but there's no one there. Ron becomes fearful of being eaten by bush animals, the fire goes out. When he resolves to act, the fire reignites. More incomprehensible words.

The fire goes out again, but he then sees firelight coming from a cave on the escarpment above. He goes to the cave fire; inside he first sees a jaguar in the firelight and is frightened. The jaguar moves, obscured by a rock, and reemerges as a most beautiful, naked woman, causing an immense erection of Ron's adolescent penis. The woman again obscured, reemerges as a jaguar who approaches the fire, rises on her haunches about to strike and again there are the incomprehensible words.

Ron, fearing death in front of him, watches as the jaguar then changes shape into a horrible-looking old crone who speaks the incomprehensible language. However, Ron now comprehends the meaning of the words, "Do not trust what you see, Trust only what you feel!" Immediately he is transported back to the first fire on the plain. His bowl is now full of food. He eats, dozes off and suddenly finds himself approaching his home.

Arriving at the threshold, he finds his grandfather who starts clapping. His grandfather's clapping is joined by the other members of the boy's family. The grandfather speaks in the incomprehensible language that Ron now understands perfectly, as do all the other members. The grandfather is saying, "Now he is a man!" over and over again.

●✧ ●✧ ●✧

Ron's father, a great shot and an avid hunter, was running oil drilling sites on newly-opened concessions in the Orinoco River delta, prime hunting country in Venezuela, especially for jaguar. His dad had the drill sites running smoothly and locating new drill sites with his expert, practiced eye and judgment, leaving great spaces of time to hunt with his son. Ron, the proverbial chip off the old block, was effectively his father's chief assistant in the oil drilling and extraction operations, as well as his hunting partner.

Being far removed from any urban centers with hunting and gun repair facilities, necessity forced Dale to be his own gunsmith and ammunition maker. As a trained petroleum and mining engineer, Dale was familiar and comfortable with high explosives and he trained Ron to be as equally proficient with guns and high explosives as he was.

Capability with explosives and firearms stood Dale and Ron in good stead since they had to provide their own security for their drill and extraction sites. The provincial police were incompetent and corrupt. The local Indians, weary of the oppression of the heirs of the *conquistadores,* had joined forces with the local communist/anarchist guerillas and bloody, but unpublicized, war prevailed in the region. Dale, a rational businessman, paid both sides to be left alone.

Dale's sympathies were with the Indians as he had a beautiful young Indian woman named Miranda as his local wife. Though married and the father of three children by Giselle, his wife in California, fidelity for Dale was wholly geographic. Giselle, ten countries and three time zones away, was not his wife in the Orinoco River delta.

At first, Ron believed that Miranda was part of the staff, but learned otherwise when he saw his father leaving his bedroom with Miranda comfortably sleeping in their bed. Seeing Ron's confusion, Dale simply told him, "In the states, your mom, Giselle, is my wife. Here, Miranda is my wife." As time went by Ron came to love and trust

Miranda as his mother and looked on her two children as his brother and sister.

His dad told Ron that while he was hunting on a nearby tributary of the Orinoco, he came upon seventeen-year-old Miranda bathing in the river. Her naked beauty dazzled him and, after she hastily dressed herself, he learned that she was a daughter of the *cacique* of the nearby Indian tribe. Dale, not playing the big shot *Norte Americano*, had excellent relations with the various Indian tribes in the area and knew Miranda's father from previous dealings with him.

Dale approached the chief regarding Miranda. Though nominally Catholic, the Indians had never given up their old gods for whom polygamy was a blessed virtue, not a sin. Dale, totally forthright, told the chief, that although he was lawfully married to Giselle in America, he wished to marry his daughter and take her as his wife.

Not blanching, the chief entered into the classical dance of marriage negotiations with Dale. Hours later, Dale emerged with the chief's blessing, and that Sunday, in a massive marriage celebration, was formally married to Miranda. The local Catholic priest, a member of Miranda's tribe, doffed his Catholic vestments, assumed the pastoral garb of a local Indian shaman and officiated at the formal tribal marriage ceremony

Ron, as Dale's son, had immediate *entrée* into Miranda's Indian family. The local Indian village became Ron's home away from home and his playground. He had the best of both worlds. At the drilling and extraction site he was the boss' son and right-hand man. At the Indian tribe, he was the step-grandson of the chief with all the rights and privileges of tribal royalty. It was better than heaven.

●◇ ●◇ ●◇

The central government of Venezuela, finally moving against the ever-bolder local insurrection, sent a newly promoted brigadier general to suppress the Indian/communist guerillas. The General had acquired a terrifying reputation as an implacable, cruel exterminator in the last anti-guerilla campaign in a neighboring province. Whole families, from infants to ancients, whose only crime was being related to a guerilla, were publicly executed. Terrified peasants informed the army of the guerillas' hiding places leading to the rebels' annihilation in that province.

The General's action plan became the model for the government's national campaign against the Indian/communist insurrection. His arrival in Dale and Ron's neighborhood was announced by a total slaughter of all the inhabitants of a small Indian village, part of Miranda's tribe. This village was located in the center of a small valley, known to be a hotbed of rebel activity. Miranda's mother was from this village, and a great number of those slaughtered were Miranda's cousins or close relatives. Ron suddenly found his new family in the midst of a war to the death left to their own devices.

They were not totally without resources. The anarcho/communists portion of the insurgency financed their large-scale insurrection with drug money from the cocaine trade. U.S. government agencies, ostensibly endeavoring to suppress and destroy the cocaine trade, in reality used portions of the indigenous cocaine trade to finance (off-the-books) their world-wide, clandestine black ops, indistinguishable from the terrorist operations of their nominal opposition.

The anarcho/communist insurgency had been turned by the ABC, the precursor to the OPL, into a cash cow for U.S. black ops. Traversing the porous borders between Bolivia, Peru, Columbia, Venezuela and Brazil, the armed anarcho/communist insurgency exacted a fabulous toll on the cocaine trade, to the point where they had a major seat on the board of directors of the South American cocaine trade.

The ABC nabbed a major figure in the anarcho/communist rebellion, and after demonstrating their resolve and capacity for horror by savagely torturing and slowly, and painfully killing his other captured comrades before his eyes, made the Jefe an offer he couldn't refuse. The U.S. would protect and support their insurrection in return for fifty percent of the insurgency's revenues from the cocaine trade. If the anarcho/communists did not agree, the U.S., in alliance with the militaries and national police of all the concerned countries, would mount a vast offensive to suppress and destroy his insurgency and deal directly with the cocaine trade themselves.

To agree meant assured income and protection from the world's superpower. To refuse meant an unwinnable war, poverty and death. The answer from the rebels was simple—fifty percent of a bonanza was better than one hundred percent of nothing—*Viva America!*

In fairness, the U.S. position was rational, albeit immoral. The U.S. cocaine market was the biggest grosser of the coke trade. The U.S. users were in the process of unalterable, self-annihilation; generating immense social costs of hospitalization, criminal conduct, incarceration, *ad nauseam*. In this way, a U.S. national objective—financing clandestine, black ops—could be attained indirectly from the actions of a population of irredeemably useless, hopelessly lost, dead-end, U.S. drug addicts. It was a Machiavellian *win-win-win* proposition. The cocaine trade would prosper, U.S. addicts would get their accustomed high at reasonable, well-supplied market purchase costs, and U.S. off-the-books financing of world-wide, clandestine black operations would occur.

The government anti-insurgency campaign hit a snag. U.S. funding of the government's anti-rebel, nation-wide extermination campaign dried up. Suddenly Ron's grandfather, the *cacique*, and his anarcho/communist allies had rifles, AK-47s, RPGs, Sidewinder anti-helicopter missiles, great supplies of all types of ammunition.

The bloody brigadier was stymied. His forays were known before they began. His columns were ambushed and his men, when not mercifully killed in combat, were hideously tortured by the Indian women, who, from times immemorial, were the torturers in the Indian wars of the Americas.

Intent on exacting revenge, The General learned from tortured Indian prisoners that the daughter of his enemy, the *cacique,* was the wife of the *Norte Americano* oilman, Dale Diamond. Notwithstanding his orders not to disturb Mr. Diamond's operations, The General, in the company of eight of his toughest hard-cases, set out for Dale and Ron's oil drilling and extraction site. They travelled by the back roads in two small armored personnel carriers, the first carrying The General and four men; with the second carrying The General's adjutant, a colonel, and four more men.

The squad seemed to be undiscovered as it approached the office and residence of Diamond Drilling. Not so! Dale's security precautions left nothing to chance. Motion sensors along the approach road noted the two personnel carriers' passage and alerted the drill operation's central security. The *cacique,* concerned for his daughter's safety, had detached fourteen men, seven coke trade rebels and seven tribesmen, to beef-up Diamond Drilling on-site security patrols. Generally these fourteen remained near the residence and office looking out for Miranda and her two young children.

Dale and Ron, out in the field, were moving at breakneck speed towards the main buildings after being alerted to the approach of the military personnel carriers.

The main building security knew of the payoff neutrality conferred on Diamond Drilling and, though at the ready, were not locked down defensively as the two personnel carriers approached. The General and the colonel, in their separate vehicles, manned the roof-mounted fifty caliber machine guns, raking the main buildings with heavy machine gun fire, killing two security guards and wounding three more.

The eight veteran soldiers expertly exited the carriers and with practiced precision were quickly subduing the remainder of the detachment. In triumph, The General and the adjutant left the dominating 50-caliber guns, to celebrate their victory with the prospective brutal torture and killing of Miranda and her two children. Dale and Ron stealthily approached from the rear, racing to the two carriers, and seized the two unattended 50-calibers. They raked the unaware soldiers with machine gun fire killing two and wounding three.

The soldiers, knowing the horrors that awaited them if they surrendered, determined to fight to the death. Realizing that the whip hand in the battle belonged to the 50-calibers, the remaining six turned to assault Dale and Ron on the roofs. Father and son coolly shot down and stood off the assaulting troopers until the avenging members of Dale's security detachment killed the grunts.

The General and his adjutant colonel fought desperately but were subdued, not killed. Payback for them would be a bitch, two bitches, in fact. When news of the capture of the The General and his colonel came to the main Indian village, Miranda's mother and aunt were overjoyed with the prospect of exacting revenge upon the two commanders who had slaughtered all their relatives and close friends in their home village. Ancient Indian tradition vested the women with the power and duty of torturing prisoners, and the two sisters relished the prospect of carrying out their duties upon The General and his aide.

As retribution, Miranda's mother and aunt, with vengeful joy, flayed the skin off The General and the colonel from their hips down. The rebels then gave them, as they screamed in agony, the coke trade's trademark, the 'Colombian Necktie,' whereby the victim's throat is slashed, his tongue is pulled out and down on his chest, silencing him while he slowly drowns in his own blood. The ten mutilated bodies were silently left that night in front of the government's military camp. Within the week, the government cancelled its campaign and abruptly pulled its troops from the province.

Fourteen-year-old Ron's bravery fighting at Dale's side in Miranda's rescue at the main buildings, turning a losing battle into victory, became legend in the province. The true victor and real party in interest, the U.S. ABC, took note of Ron's cool courage and resolution, marking him down as a "comer." In addition, Ron's cold-blooded reaction while observing the torture death of The General and his adjutant was noted by the ABC as a useful attribute for a potential black operations agent. Young

Ron was one to follow as he grew up and to encourage his further useful development.

All dreams end. So did Ron's Venezuelan idyll. For Ron to become an engineer like his dad, he'd have to finish high school in the U.S. to get into college. Suddenly, he was just a sixteen-year-old high school junior, living with his mother, Giselle, in El Cerrito, California, helping after-school and weekends at her busy, prospering 7-11 store on San Pablo Avenue. A far cry from being Dale's drill site assistant and tribal royalty in the village.

•◊ •◊ •◊

Having no school records to speak of, Ron was placed by the El Cerrito school district in the 1967 junior class of his local, neighborhood high school, Madison.

"Ron, get going! You're going to be late, again," yelled his mom, Giselle.

"Geez, Mom, let it be. I'm gone!" Ron shouted, as he slammed the door.

Ron was now sixteen, a big, muscular, Nordic-type, whose ancestral origins were from all parts of the Baltic Sea—Norway, Sweden, Estonia and Prussia. His family arrived in Minnesota, stayed for one generation, then wanderlust reasserted itself and they were gone to the mines of California and places south. Mining engineering was in the blood. Three generations of Diamonds before Ron were mining engineers. Ron had the genetic predilection in spades and took to mining like a duck to water.

Dale, his father, did not totally abandon him to the wolves when he sent him home to school. He outfitted the family home with a complete machine shop to enable Ron to continue to develop his engineering and gunsmith skills. He also bought him a used, six-year old Mustang hardtop convertible for him to fix-up and romance the honeys.

The months before school started, after working at Mom's 7-11, Ron spent all his time fixing up his car. When Ron rolled into the school's parking lot on the first day with a beautiful, iridescent black Mustang with cherry-red highlights, the girls swarmed like ants to a picnic. Charming them with the social skills developed as Dale's #2 in Venezuela, Ron honed in on Barbara—a petite blonde with a beautiful face and a knock-out body, possessing an animated, challenging wit and demeanor—a real tiger.

Barbara had some baggage, however. His name was Buddy (given name Robert). Buddy was Barbara's nominal boyfriend. Nominal in the sense that, while Barbara was supposed to be monogamous, Buddy, the varsity star halfback, was free to pursue whatever other girls that he pleased, including Barbara's former best friend, Natalie. Buddy's adventure with Natalie, starting in July, concluded just before Labor Day, when he purportedly returned to Barbara, but she was having none of it. Nonetheless, Buddy still considered Barbara to be HIS girlfriend.

When word got out about Ron and Barbara's hook-up, Buddy was enraged, not so much at losing Barbara but at losing face in school. This new kid, Ron, having no background or reputation, and possessing only a hot-looking car, needed to be taught his place in the pecking order at Madison High School. Word of Buddy's planned revenge spread along Madison's grapevine, reaching Barbara, who, knowing Buddy's mean streak, warned Ron.

Ron's time spent at his father's Venezuela oil drilling sites gave him great expertise in offensive and defensive security measures. After Barbara's warning he wore his steel work boots to school and carried a sap—a leather pouch filled with five rolls of quarters—in his jacket pocket. Thursday after school Ron and Barbara were in the parking lot, approaching Ron's car, when they saw Buddy with two football teammates at Ron's car.

Buddy's friends were the large, bulky offensive tackle, and the large, muscular tight end. As usual, the parking lot was full of kids and their parents. Buddy, an arrogant jock hero, wanted to make sure everyone saw Ron's denigration. Seeing Barbara with Ron, Buddy, with a snarl, shouted:

"Hey Ron, you sonofabitch, you took Barbara, and now I'm taking your car down!"

"Buddy, you pathetic, useless pindick, I've finally found a guy worth having. Get lost!" yelled Barbara, at the top of her lungs. Enraged, Buddy, holding a baseball bat, knocked out Ron's headlights and taillights and was proceeding to smash the front and rear glass windshields, when Ron moved to defend his Mustang.

Buddy's two teammates menacingly advanced towards the onrushing Ron. With blazing speed, Ron, in a left-handed backwards slash, unlimbered his sap filled with five rolls of quarters savagely against the left side of the tackle's face breaking his cheekbone, jawbone, and causing his left eye to bulge and nearly fall out of its socket. Ron, without breaking stride, ferociously kicked the tight end's left shin with his steel-toed boot, causing compound fractures of his left tibia and fibula, immediately dropping him to the ground, screaming and writhing in agony. Now, it was Buddy's turn.

Buddy's cocksure confidence in his teammates' protection evaporated in a horrifying instant. Disabled and savagely injured, they would provide no help; in fact they were in desperate need of emergency medical care. Was this unknown Ron a demon from hell? With no time to think, Buddy had to defend himself. Ron face was a terrifying sight; calm, cold and relentless, his eyes empty and flat. His was the face of Death.

Buddy tried to use the baseball bat to disable Ron. Using both his hands, he took a couple of bat strokes aimed at Ron's head and upper body. Buddy whiffed badly. On the second stroke's follow-through, Ron stripped the bat from his hands with a blow from his sap.

Now Buddy was at Ron's mercy. There was none to be found.

Although Buddy and Ron were approximately the same height and build, the advantage was wholly with Ron. His Venezuela experience had made him a warrior. In a fight, he was a killer without remorse. In abject terror, Buddy turned and began running as fast as he could. Buddy was renowned as a blazingly fast half-back, capable of outrunning all pursuit on a football field, but the parking lot was no football field—there were no referees, no rulebook, and Ron was not a sportsman.

With preternatural quickness, Ron caught up with Buddy from behind, knocked him down face first on the asphalt, shattering Buddy's beautiful aquiline nose and splitting both his lips on the flat asphalt. Turning Buddy over Ron smiled when he saw the disaster that was Buddy's face. The nose and lips would heal relatively quickly, not so the other injury.

Inadvertently Buddy suffered a severely broken right hand and wrist trying to brace his fall. Buddy's Pac 10 football scholarship depended upon his senior season's performance. Buddy, the star halfback, carried the ball with his right hand. The shattered bones of his right wrist and fingers effectively ended Buddy's senior football season and his hoped-for athletic scholarship.

In the hubbub that followed, the parking lot full of witnesses, led by Pat, the PTA's Secretary-Treasurer (also the mother of Natalie, Barbara's former best friend) all stated the three football players were the fight's instigators. The jock bullies had badly miscalculated. Their designated victim, Ron, was no meek lamb, but a David who slew three Goliaths.

After investigating the incident, Buddy and his two teammates were charged with conspiracy, assault and battery and malicious mischief. At the jury trial, Ron and Barbara were dynamite witnesses. Barbara was the quintessence of the sweet high school girl, while Ron was every mother's ideal of a stalwart, self-reliant son. Given the number of reputable parking lot eyewitnesses for the prosecution, Buddy and his two accomplices had short shrift at trial. The jury was out for twenty minutes, barely enough time to select a foreperson and take one guilty verdict ballot.

Ron became an instant hero to all the students who were fed up with the stifling dominance of Madison High's entrenched jock culture. As an increasingly negative spin evolved about the controlling student elite, Ron and Barbara became the twin rallying points of an unstoppable groundswell to topple the jocks. After Ron and Barb were selected the spring's junior prom king and queen, Ron ran for and won election as student body president for his upcoming senior year, ending decades of control by the jock/cheerleader social elite.

Besides county jail time, the three players had to make restitution to Ron for the bat damage Buddy did to the Mustang. The three's crying and moaning about their injuries were dismissed and regarded by the jury and the sentencing judge as a proper punishment for their outrageous conduct. As a final blow, since the three had skipped football practice to attack Ron, the Madison football coach threw all three players off the football team. With the ironic cruelty that comes naturally to high school, the three got new Madison nicknames—"Lefty" (Buddy), "Popeye" (the tackle), and "Gimpy" (the end).

Lefty, Popeye and Gimpy, all got jail time. After two weeks, Popeye and Gimpy, Lefty's dupes, got probation with credit for time served. Lefty (Buddy) as the instigating mastermind was facing, at the very least, four more months of solid jail time. Once Lefty lost Popeye and Gimpy's beefy jailhouse protection, he became fresh meat for the depravity of the other jail inmates.

Two days after Popeye and Gimpy were released on probation, Lefty was knocked down onto the shower floor and sodomized multiple times by a massive, brutal inmate. Lefty/Buddy was in terror. Later, a member of the inmate gang controlling the jail, who witnessed his shower rape, asked Buddy if he wanted revenge. Buddy, beside himself with rage, screamed his desire for vengeance. Buddy was advised if he showered at the same time tomorrow, his desired revenge would be granted.

The next morning at 8:15 am, Buddy went into the shower. The sodomizer from the day before followed him, looking for a replay of his fun. Not so today. When he made a move toward Buddy, immediately tattooed members of the inmate gang grabbed and spread-eagled him on the shower floor. Buddy was handed a "shank", a strip of sharpened metal, used as a makeshift knife or razor in jail, and told to take his revenge.

Buddy stabbed his rapist in the scrotum and twisted the shank, causing the rapist's testicles to spew out onto the shower floor and, with a towel stuffed in the now terrified rapist's mouth, stifling his agonized screams, cut his throat from ear to ear, killing him. Buddy was now entitled to have one teardrop tattooed on his cheek near his eye, as a memento of his kill. No longer was Ron the only warrior, now Buddy could match Ron's cold, relentless warrior demeanor and attitude.

The inmate gang's interest in Buddy was not altruistic. Their outside members needed an opening for drug sales at Madison high and its student body. Buddy, the football hero, would give them their entrée to Madison. Buddy's active and voluntary cooperation with the gang was necessary to accomplish their goal. Turning Buddy into a loyal gang member was required. No better way existed than to make Buddy dependent on the gang's protection.

A brutal, huge homosexual jail inmate, who relished forcible sodomy, was causing the gang no end of trouble. The gang indirectly encouraged him to forcibly sodomize Buddy in the shower. The shower rape played into their hands, for it enabled them to dispose of a vicious, queer rapist, and, by such act, to forever bind Buddy to the gang.

After his revenge, Buddy was grateful and, by the killing, perpetually liable for prosecution for the shower murder. Buddy's loyalty to the gang was ensured as they controlled all the witnesses and possessed the murder weapon. Again, it was a *win-win-win* proposition—by getting Buddy his revenge, the gang was rid of a dangerous troublemaker and developed Buddy into a dependent, new member who, when sprung, could access the rich, untapped potential drug market at El Cerrito's Madison High.

The high school district had a tutorial instruction program for its students hospitalized or sentenced to jail. The program sought to prevent dropouts and ensure that its disabled or jailed students graduated on time. The program relied on student volunteers, friends of the absent student, to bring assignments to her/him and return completions to school.

Popeye and Gimpy volunteered to bring Lefty his assignments at jail. These visits also allowed unsupervised contact between the three students. Popeye and Gimpy told Lefty/Buddy of the successful onslaught of Ron and Barbara to destroy the jock social elite, culminating in Ron's election as student body president for his upcoming senior year. Buddy, feeling responsible for this terrible turn of events, vowed to make Ron's senior year particular hell.

Buddy religiously completed all his assignments, insuring that he would graduate on time with his senior class. He told Popeye and Gimpy of his intent to make big bucks after graduation in drug sales, capitalizing on the changing drug attitudes of the late sixties. As Popeye and Gimpy had no college plans, they joined with Buddy's initiative. Buddy introduced them to his gang mentors in jail, who knowing Popeye and Gimpy from their two-week jail stint, approved their participation as members of Buddy/Lefty's crew.

When Buddy completed his jail time at the end of May, he went back to Madison for the last week before graduation. When he returned, the defeated jock/cheerleader social elite welcomed him back as their tested battle commander coming to rally his troops and recapture the school. That was not Lefty's plan, but he encouraged his supporters to continue the fight. His intent was to prepare the field for his new drug sales endeavor beginning immediately after graduation in mid-June.

After Buddy's shower revenge, the inmate gang sanitized the murder scene, protecting their newfound asset. To be truthful, the jail guards didn't make much of an investigative effort as they, like the inmates, generally loathed the dead predator. The consensus feeling was, "Good riddance to bad rubbish!" One consequence surprised Buddy. He enjoyed killing his rapist and joyfully relived, in his memory, the murder's details over and over again. He decided to forever abandon "Buddy" and now went by his jail name—"Lefty."

The acquisition, merchandising and sales of pot, coke, heroin, LSD and meth to the Madison High market were to be handled by the gang's outside sales professionals. Lefty, Popeye and Gimpy were to be the party-throwers bringing their vapid, self-indulgent jock/cheerleader elite friends to "A" list parties where sex, drugs and rock and roll was the only standard to be satisfied.

Lefty's pull as the jock's leader brought all Madison's beautiful people to their summer parties at the condo with pool that the gang rented for Lefty's use. The plan worked out better than hoped. By late summer, the Madison High jock/cheerleader elite were copious users of all drug types, generating rich returns. Lefty's stock with the gang rose to new heights.

With his new status, Lefty made an unusual request—that he and his crew of Popeye and Gimpy be the gang's enforcers for any problems arising with the Madison clientele. The request was granted. Lefty was not only Bacchus, the party-giver, but also Mars, the god of war, in the Madison High drug scene. Now Lefty was positioned to wreak particular hell upon Ron and Barbara for their "crimes" of forever ruining Buddy's college football scholarship dreams.

●◇ ●◇ ●◇

Ron's return to his El Cerrito home to finish high school was successful beyond all expectations. From a friendless, unknown high school junior, he rocketed to senior class student-body president with Barb, the queen of the junior prom, as his girlfriend. His luck was too good to last, and it didn't.

After his triumphant election as senior class president, Ron's parents rewarded him with a summer's vacation trip to Venezuela to his father's home and flourishing business on the Orinoco River. Having avenged the sack and massacre of Miranda's mother's village by the defeat and killing of The General, Ron's father, Dale, was given exclusive hunting rights in the valley where the destroyed village formerly stood. It was a great gift to avid hunters Dale and Ron for the forest and savannah around that village were renowned as rich hunting country teeming with game and jaguar.

Rich hunting country also attracts natural predators, such as anaconda and a particularly lethal six-foot-long poisonous black snake, called the Messenger of Death. The immense anaconda's legendary ability to squeeze and swallow whole animals and persons was known world-wide, not so much the Messenger's lethal nature. Predators, such as snakes, generally limit their killing skills to hunting food and self-defense. The MoD, of course, killed for food and self-defense, but also killed animals and persons apparently for the pure pleasure of the kill—a naturally psychopathic snake. This dread attribute was known by the local Indians who gave, when possible, the MoD a wide berth. The MoD's favorite killing gambit was to wait up in the overhanging tree branches, dropping down without warning on selected prey, animal or human, injecting its victim with a universally fatal bite and leaving it to die a slow, agonizing death without attempting to feed upon it.

One exceptionally gorgeous hunting day, at mid-morning, Dale and Ron were moving abreast across a forested savannah seeking to flush game by their maneuver. Ron, impetuous and impatient, had perceptively distanced himself ahead of Dale. His father, focusing on flushing game from the bush in front of him, looked over to check on Ron's progress ahead of him. In horror, Dale saw a MoD in the branches above immediately in front of Ron, poised to drop upon Ron and kill him.

Dale yelled a warning to Ron, who, focused on the bush in front of him, was unaware of the snake poised to strike him from the branches above. Dropping his rifle, Dale raced to Ron and threw his body over Ron, covering him from the plummeting MoD, and taking the fatal bite himself. Shocked by Dale's saving tackle, Ron quickly recovered and killed the MoD with a stroke from his bush-clearing machete. The MoD had delivered his message of death to Dale. Within minutes Dale was no more.

Ron was bereft. Dale, his dad, mentor, idol and protector—was gone forever. Ron felt frightened and alone. The province was stricken with the news, as Dale had become a local hero. Dale's business interests were disposed of in probate pursuant to his Will, that provided equally well for Miranda and her children as well as for Giselle and her brood.

Word of Dale's death and Ron's final return to Northern California passed from Miranda's father, the cacique, to his rebel comrades, who passed the word on to their patrons, the U.S. ABC drug agency. The word went back to ABC's D.C. headquarters with a watch memo sent to their local officer in western Contra Costa County, to keep an eye on Ron for possible future recruitment and use.

Because of a close working relationship developed with Mal Boldt, area deputy D.A. for the El Cerrito judicial district, the local watch officer Jim FitzGibbon contacted Mal Boldt and informed him of his agency's interest in Ron Diamond.

After Buddy dumped her, Natalie, Barb's former best friend, took up with Phil McAuliffe, a junior on the football team who inherited Gimpy's starting tight end position. He did so well that he was selected to the all-league team as an end and received intense football recruitment interest from various college teams. He was one of the leading lights of the defeated jock/cheerleader social elite, who flocked that summer to Lefty's condo for drug parties.

Natalie, as Phil's girlfriend, was at all the summer drug parties at Lefty's condo. By nature a star-fucker, Natalie still had the hots for Lefty (formerly Buddy) dismissing his cruel sexual use and casual discarding of her a year earlier. Now that he had transcended his shame and was a rich and powerful party giver at his condo with unlimited access to the new in-thing, drugs, she wanted him even more.

Natalie had filled out nicely. Her unremarkable breasts had turned the corner and become sexy with tempting décolletage. Her long thin legs received the benediction of full, rounded thighs and well-turned calves and ankles. Her face now was not so much cute as classically angular with provocative green eyes and full lips. In short, she had turned into a young beauty, albeit vapid and shallow.

Having finally escaped, totally, the chrysalis of puberty and come into the noonday sun of full hormonal sexual desire, Natalie's lust, not too well-hidden, manifested itself quickly. With Phil, as alpha-male, surrounded by the other female groupies in the jock/cheerleader elite who, without words, by glances and innuendo promised Phil all pleasures of the flesh within their province to command, Natalie was free to direct her attentions to her target of choice, Lefty, the rich god of parties, drugs and youthful independence.

Lefty, remembering his earlier liaison with Natalie, was struck by the physical change in her appearance and demeanor. His earlier dalliance with Natalie was primarily in the realm of a sexual wine tasting. As Barb's acknowledged boyfriend, he was aware of Natalie, as Barb's best friend, always hanging around. Barb, witty and voluptuous, was more than sufficient for his sexual needs but one gets tired of a diet of filet mignon and vintage champagne and sometimes has a craving for hot dogs and beer.

Natalie, a year earlier, satisfied his consuming, insatiable craving for hot dogs and beer, sexually speaking. Then Natalie's body, wit and brains did not measure up to Barb's, but her pussy, boobs and bedroom performance looked, smelled, tasted and felt different and that was more than enough to keep him interested for six weeks until the novelty wore off. Tragically, when Lefty wanted to return to Barb's more elegant and substantial sexual fare, Ron had come on the scene and the rest, from Lefty's standpoint, was disastrous history.

Now as Madison High's drug czar, party-giver, supplier and enforcer—Lefty had a new attractiveness. Power has always been a natural aphrodisiac to women and it was no different now. The sexual attractiveness of Buddy, the campus football hero, couldn't hold a candle to the attraction of Lefty, the indulgent, rich drug lord, to his clientele, the jock/cheerleader elite. Natalie, the new, beautiful edition, was his for the asking. "Ask and ye shall receive," and Lefty did, in spades!

Lefty and Natalie's sexual reconciliation and homecoming were celebrated at Lefty's rental, miles from the El Cerrito drug party condo. Lefty, with his portion of the drug proceeds, had rented a shoreline bungalow at Point Richmond. Point Richmond, though not generally well known, had a spectacular view of San Francisco and the Marin headlands nestled at the base of steep rock formation that insulates it from the Chevron Refinery and the urban travails of Richmond proper. Lefty's bungalow had a pier going into San Pablo Bay with a speedboat moored there. It was an idyllic setting of which Lefty and Natalie took full blissful advantage during their reunion.

After exhausting each other with their youthful sexual exuberance, the topic of Barbara and Ron came up. Surprisingly, it was first broached by Natalie. When Barbara first heard of Buddy's infidelity with Natalie, she was not so much angry with Buddy as livid with rage at the betrayal by her lifelong best friend. From being the closest of friends, Barbara and Natalie immediately went to a deep, abiding hatred and loathing of each other.

As time went on, the enmity did not dissipate but increased at an almost geometric rate. After Buddy discarded her, coupled with the disastrous parking lot revenge attack that led to Barb and Ron's triumphant overthrow of the jock elite, Natalie found herself shunned and ostracized at school. Natalie's thirst for revenge upon Barb and Ron found an equally intense response in Lefty.

Ron's Achilles' heel was his mother Giselle's 7-11 store near Madison High, where he worked daily after school. With his father's tragic hunting death etched in his memory, Ron became very protective of his mother's vulnerability as owner-clerk at her store. Barb generally accompanied Ron daily to his mom's store. Within a week she also was on the store's payroll with Ron, having the same scheduled hours.

The presence of the jointly popular Barb and Ron at the 7-11 store near the high school brought a palpable increase in the store's patronage from Madison. With the onset of the drug culture at Madison, primarily due to

Lefty's parties, Lefty's sellers tried to use the 7-11 location to sell drugs. Ron, alert to the drug usage and their source, rousted the traffickers out of his mom's store and called the cops.

As the drug gang's Madison enforcers, Lefty's crew was directed to eliminate Ron's interference and open up Giselle's 7-11 to their drug sales. Lefty now had three reasons to take immediate revenge upon Ron and Barbara—his own and Natalie's rage and the directive of his criminal bosses. Determined not only to kill Ron but to terrorize him, Lefty planned to rape and kill Giselle and Barbara at the 7-11 in front of Ron before Lefty killed Ron.

Dutifully he advised his drug leaders of the planned triple murder scenario to carry out their directive. Leadership, not shy of bloodletting when necessary to further their ends, rejected Lefty's planned triple murder as over the top and likely to lead to police war, destroying their lucrative Madison market. Lefty was summarily told to stop and threatened with harsh sanctions if he continued. Lefty, finally about to realize his long-desired revenge upon Ron and Barbara, rejected the gang's order and confirmed his intent to carry out his planned murderous revenge.

The gang quietly contacted Popeye and Gimpy, the other members of Lefty's crew, to advise them of their prohibition of his planned triple murders. By this time, Gimpy and Popeye had become very happy with their lucrative drug gang connection and would do nothing to offend their paymasters, the drug lords. It was hinted that perhaps Popeye or Gimpy should "drop a dime" to law enforcement, warning of Lefty's planned triple murders.

Popeye and Gimpy recalled Mal Boldt, the El Cerrito area District Deputy Attorney, who tried and convicted all three of them for the school parking lot assault on Ron a year earlier. Mal Boldt, from his participation in the trial and sentencing, knew all the players and would not need extensive background review. A "dime was dropped" on Lefty to Mal Boldt.

Mal Boldt, independently informed of the opening of the Madison High drug scene, contacted Jim FitzGibbon, his acquaintance in ABC's office. He told Fitz about everything, especially of the information Mal Boldt had just received of the planned triple murders. Fitz reviewed ABC files and came across Ron as a potential recruiting prospect on their D.C. watch list based upon his Venezuela activities. After his record search, FitzGibbon told Mal Boldt that his office was interested and asked to be included in all further aspects of this case.

Ron received a telephone message from Mal Boldt at his mom's store. He recognized his voice and recalled that Mal Boldt was the District D.A. who successfully prosecuted and won the criminal jury verdict against Buddy and his two football friends for their parking lot assault and battery upon him. Mal Boldt stated that he needed to make a follow-up report concerning Buddy and his friends and set a Thursday 3:30 pm appointment at the Contra Costa County D.A.'s Richmond branch office.

When Ron arrived, Mal introduced him to FitzGibbon. This was to be the first of many meetings over the years between Ron and Fitz.

In the course of that first interview, Ron was told of Buddy/Lefty's heavy involvement in drug sales to Madison High students. Ron, on info from his friends, coupled with run-ins with Lefty's pushers at his mom's store, already had that information and more.

When told of the Lefty's intended rape/murders of Giselle and Barb and his own murder, Ron was incredulous, then angry and concerned. Breaking his silence, Fitz told Ron his agency was impressed with his prior Venezuela activities and would take any and all measures necessary to protect Ron, Giselle and Barb from Lefty's homicidal plans. Quickly remembering ABC's protective alliance with the Venezuela rebels, Ron requested a pistol, hollow-point ammo and an unlimited pistol use permit giving him federal peace officer status.

Without a murmur, Jim FitzGibbon agreed and suggested they meet tomorrow at a place more appropriate than the D.A.'s branch office to transfer the requested items. Mal Boldt interjected, stating he couldn't participate further, and excused himself from the next day's transfer meeting. Ron and Jim agreed to meet Friday in the back pool table room at the infamous Wagon Wheel Restaurant in the unincorporated no-man's land nestled in between the Richmond and El Cerrito city limits at the quiet time of 2:30 p.m.

The next day at Madison, Ron told Barb that he'd be two hours late at his mother's because he had very important private meeting at The Wagon Wheel Restaurant. Natalie, nearby, overheard this and, in her regular noontime telephone call to Lefty, mentioned it in passing to him. Lefty, alert to his chance to kill Ron without witnesses, without informing Natalie or anyone else, determined to go that afternoon to the Wagon Wheel armed to kill Ron.

Lefty arrived the Wagon Wheel Restaurant at 3:00 pm, shortly after Fitz transferred the loaded pistol and the federal gun permit to Ron. Lefty burst into the nearly-empty back pool table room brandishing his pistol, threatening to rape and murder Giselle and Barb after he killed Ron. Lefty had miscalculated badly; Ron was in a murderous rage and better armed.

Ron, adrenalin flooding his body, was unstoppable. He grabbed Lefty and threw him heavily upon the slate covered, concrete pool table, momentarily stunning him. While Lefty was stunned, Ron deliberately took out his pistol, placed it against Lefty's head, pulled the trigger twice, blowing his brains all over the leather pool table covering. Jim, with a slow smile, went to Ron, took back the pistol and the federal gun permit, giving Ron a congratulatory pat on his shoulder. Stating he'd take care of the situation, Jim arranged a quiet, surreptitious cleanup of the bloody mess that formerly was Lefty.

Ultimately Lefty arranged for his own body's disappearance. Making use of Lefty's speedboat at his

Point Richmond pier, Lefty's body was securely weighted down, dumped at rip tide in the Bay near the Golden Gate Bridge and taken out by the tide to the Pacific Ocean where Lefty would forever "sleep with the fishes."

Agent Jim FitzGibbon was astounded how cool and calm Ron was during the cleanup and disposal of Lefty's body. He noted that Ron, as a matter of fact, said he was starving, went to a restaurant for dinner, had a voracious appetite and carried on a rational, intelligent conversation about other things during and after dinner. Jim reported to headquarters that Ron Diamond was a blue-chip acquisition—a five-tool player, a future black-ops Hall-of-Famer—unflappable, relentless and unfailingly lethal.

To ensure Ron's full cooperation with their future plans for him, agent FitzGibbon, on behalf of the ABC, retained the pistol, the ammunition and the permit. The gun, ammo, and permit, coupled with pictures and reports of the killing location and the disposal of Lefty's body discreetly taken and compiled, were safely filed away at ABC's high security storage facility in Utah.

What bound Lefty to the inmate gang—that no statute of limitations exists on murders—also acted to forever bind Ron to the government, the ABC and whatever federal agencies later came into the picture. Ron didn't realize it yet, but he was now owned lock, stock and barrel by the U.S. government. He'd better be a good, obedient soldier or the maximum-security federal prisons at Leavenworth or Atlanta would beckon him home.

Maya Mitra Das

Poet and short story writer Maya Mitra Das was born in India and came to the U.S. in 1973. She studied internal medicine and pediatrics in India, England and the United States, earning her M.D. and Ph.D. She received her training at Downstate Medical Center and State University Hospital in Brooklyn, New York.

She completed two fellowships—one for the department of hematology and oncology at U.C.L.A. Medical Center and the second at University of California San Francisco for radiation oncology. She currently serves on the medical staff at Children's Hospital in Oakland, California working with sickle cell anemia in children.

Among many hobbies, Maya performs 'Bharatnatyam' Indian classical dance. Her poetry has appeared in *Tuesday's Poetry*, edited by Jerry Ball, two narrative poems have been anthologized in *What's in a Name*, edited by Elaine Starkman and she has also authored several scientific publications. Her fiction is based on true events in her mother's life with Mahatma Gandhi before independence in India.

The House by the Creek

◆

Noyakhali, an idyllic town in the east part of
undivided Bengal in India, lay in a fertile landscape
surrounded by tall palm and coconut trees whispering in
the gentle breeze. Above the land stretched a dome of
blue sky that descended to kiss the golden paddy fields as
river and creeks danced along side by side.

There were houses big and small nestled around
the landscape where Hindus and Muslims lived happily
sharing bonds and close ties with each other. The
neighbors, who had mutual generosity and respect for
each other, celebrated their festivals and religious rites
without consequence.

The political landscape in 1946, when a storm of
communal riots blew over the eastern part of Bengal and
the western part of Punjab in India before India gained
independence, told a different story. With the riots came a
wave of terrorism that swept along with it both death and
destruction.

Mahatma Gandhi arrived with a peace mission to
Noyakhali feeling optimistic that his presence would have
a calming effect. He visited the towns and villages in the
area, section by section, daily treading unpaved and
muddy paths. As always, Gandhi walked in front of his
followers wearing his signature attire striding firmly with
his walking stick.

One of the followers was a young journalist, Bimal, who on one such daily tour, accompanied Gandhi and his group down a narrow, muddy path, which led through the paddy fields and curved toward a pond where blossoming lilies' sweet fragrances scented the air.

A scorched granary sitting desolate in the shade of trees popped its head while the surrounding coconut trees sighed with the breeze. Nearby a charred house creaked in a blast of wind and a burnt smell filled the air as Gandhi passed by. The creaking sound of the burned house continued as if it wanted to be acknowledged.

Way past a turn in the road, a house that was not damaged but standing elegantly by the creek surrounded by lush greeneries featured all varieties of fruit trees like mangos, lychees, and jackfruit. There was also a vegetable garden and a medium-size pond for edible fish. The pink lilies that graced the pond seemed to have a story to tell.

The wooden carved door at the front of the house stood half open. An aura that surrounded the house affected the group of visitors with a feeling of uneasiness. The group stopped and looked at each other.

Gandhi turned to the young journalist in the group. "Bimal, is this the house?"

Bimal came forward, his head down. "Yes, Bapujee."

As the father of the nation, Gandhi was accustomed to being fondly called "Bapujee" by all Indians.

Gandhi motioned for Bimal to take the lead as it was the journalist's desire to see and write down every thing exactly "as it is no less or no more." As he entered the house, Bimal felt that it might have been recently occupied but that its occupants may have left in a hurry. The living room furniture was moved, a table was upside down, and pieces of broken sculpture lay strewn on the floor. A painting on the wall was crooked, one lacy curtain was torn, and there were rust-colored footprints on the floor.

Bimal continued walking through the house along a hallway leading to the kitchen on one side and the bedrooms on the other. The smell of cooking spices still lingered in the air; one person from the group took a deep breath and said, "Someone must have been cooking here not too long ago."

Across the hallway were several bedrooms. Two of the medium-size bedroom closets were flung open and women's garments like saris of different designs and colors were strewn on the floor. Petticoats designed to wear underneath a sari and blouses to match the saris were scattered across the floor and furniture. In one of the bedrooms, the pillows and bed sheets had been torn and lay in heaps over broken furniture and shattered photographs.

While Bimal was taking photos of this scene someone from the group called him from the master bedroom and Bimal ran to see what was going on. Before him lay a ghastly scene of splattered bloodstains on the walls and as well as the ceiling. Long streaks of dried out blood that stained the walls made his skin crawl. The carved wooden headboard of the bed bore a similar stain. The bed sheets were pulled from the bed, as were the pillows. Pieces of rope lay on the bed.

Controlling his emotion, Bimal summoned and guided Gandhi to the room.

"Bapujee, these are all blood stained images." Bimal's voice echoed feelings of grief and despair. "I understand, people have drowned themselves in the sea of hatred and rage."

Gandhi shook his head sadly.

At that moment, a golden retriever ran into the room whimpering as it sat near Gandhi's feet, as if the dog knew who Gandhi was. The group was moved in tears by the devastation in the room even without knowing what had happened.

A man from the neighborhood then entered the room, knelt down at Gandhi's feet and started crying pitifully. He felt compelled to share what he witnessed but he was choking with fear and sadness. Bapujee assured the man he was safe now and encouraged him to tell his story.

"A day before yesterday around midnight, I heard a group of people shouting Allah's name," the man said, breathing heavily. "They were carrying fire torches and surrounded this house—the house of Sarkar Babu, my neighbor. Then, I heard awful noises as if the house was being invaded and broken into."

The man paused to wipe his eyes.

"Then I heard screams of a woman's voice and realized it was the lady of house calling for help. I've known Sarkar Babu and his family for a long time, but I felt helpless. I could not do anything."

The man said that according to Sarkar Babu's daughter, Nandini, who knocked on his door very early the next morning, there were several attackers armed with swords and bamboo sticks. "I am fearful even now and ask for help. If the attackers know that I speak to you now, they will harm me and my family. I am a Muslim. My name is Rahim. Sarkar Babu and his family have been close friends of mine for a long time."

He said that Nandini looked very pale and trembled uncontrollably from her ordeal. "Her clothes were wet and dripping with water. She told me that she hid herself in the pond and managed to survive by holding onto the moss and the lilies. Nandini cried out loud and said, 'The attacker's decapitated Baba (Father) in front of my Ma and started playing soccer using his head as a ball.' "

The man's body shook as he recalled Nandini's chilling account: "Ma screamed in terror until they stuffed torn pieces of cloth in her mouth and tied her with a rope. Then, she fainted. Thinking she was dead, the men carried her and threw her in the bushes, near the rice paddies. One of them started pulling my clothes off while another slapped me and yanked my hair. I kept screaming and my faithful dog, Bahadur jumped on the attackers and started to bite them. So the men tried to fight off Bahadur, trying to kill him but my dog ferociously attacked back. During the struggle, I escaped. I later heard my dog barking, so thankfully, he managed to also escape through a stairway to the roof. The dog saved my life."

Bimal shook his head as he listened to the man's story. "Rahim, where is the girl now and does anyone know what happened to the mother?"

Rahim cowered, as if he was afraid of being discovered by the attackers. "Bapujee, I am worried and scared to tell what else I know."

Bapujee took his hand and assured him that he and his group would try to help him as much they could.

"Nandini begged me for help," Rahim continued. "So I went out with her to search for her mother in the rice paddies. Luckily, her mother was still alive, badly bruised, but thankfully, still alive. I carried the mother back to my home as Nandini followed. My wife, Shelma, gave them tea and dry clothes.

"I offered them shelter in my home and asked them to put on *burkas* to conceal their identity. They rested through the heat of the day. After midnight, I asked my friend who has a bullock cart to take them to our doctor's house where they could be safe for a short time. They boarded that cart hiding behind the load of rice bags and were taken to the safety of the doctor's home. Before leaving, Nandini asked if I could arrange passage for them to Calcutta. They had relatives who lived in the vicinity who would offer them a place to stay for now. Before Nandini left, she asked if I could take good care of her loyal dog, Bahadur, to whom she's grateful to for saving her life. I assured her that I would be honored. A hero like Bahadur deserves a good home."

Rahim paused briefly from recounting the tragic events that had befallen his neighbors. "Tell me, Bapujee, who started this? Why we are in misery? We used to live here peacefully and in harmony with each other."

Gandhi sighed as he placed his hand over Rahim's head. "We have to be strong together and stand firm against this senseless riot."

Gandhi called Nirmal, one of his loyal followers to arrange a secure passage for Nandini and her mother to ensure their safe destination. Nirmal responded that he would arrange the medical supply truck to pick them up from where they were staying and take them to Ferry Ghat (the docking station) near the city of Dacca. There they would board an early ride by boat and then take a train directly to Calcutta.

"I will arrange for someone to accompany them to make sure they reach their destination safely," Nirmal said.

Rahim wanted to accompany Nirmal to see Nandini and her mother, Shobha Devi, whom he fondly referred to as Bhabijee, a term of endearment used to call an elder brother's wife, for the last time.

The next morning, while it was still dark, Rahim and the truck driver picked up Nandini and her mother. The stars still shone and the day was drawn with a pale light brush in the eastern sky. Under the crescent moon, a few birds began their early songs as they fluttered their wings.

As promised, the boat sat waiting in the water, carrying the hope for survival not just for Nandini and her mother but for future generations. Rahim bid farewell to his neighbors and friends and wished them a safe journey. Before their departure, Nandini once again made sure that Rahim would take good care of Bahadur. Nirmal said that he would do his best to send the dog with a medical supply person to Calcutta, perhaps later after Shobha Devi and Nandini have settled, if they wished. Despite their grief over losing the patriarch of their household, the women were overjoyed at the prospect of seeing their faithful dog, who had become a beloved member of their family.

Nandini and her mother got into the boat and soon it slowly moved away from shore as Rahim stood on the bank of the river watching them.

His figure grew even smaller with each stroke of the oars. Nandini and her mother, still wearing those all-concealing *burkas*, watched the sad, but relieved face of Rahim disappear in the distance.

Much later, when Nandini and Shobha Devi reached the train station, there were people waiting for them wearing Red Cross badges. One of them was a nurse. They boarded the train and were escorted to a compartment occupied by Red Cross workers.

The train whistled and pushed forward. The mother and daughter, despite their recent trauma, felt a magical protection around them as the train gathered speed and whizzed through countryside, leaving behind their once blissful home. They looked around them, at the nurse and other volunteers whose smiles warmed their hearts. Assured by their newfound safety net, Nandini and her mother removed the *burkas* and hugged each other tightly.

After wiping their tears of grief and relief, they turned to face the train windows as their hearts raced faster and faster with the uncertainty of the unknown. While still numb from their tragedy, they found comfort by holding hands. As the distance from there home grew greater, they cried out loud for the first time, but it would be a long time before they would find peace from their pain.

Manjari and The Ballad of Peace

❧

The sun sank slowly beyond the horizon as the last glow of the day flooded the fields and the valleys. The tall "Shaal" and "Pyall" trees started to move their limbs with the gentle breeze. The "Sonajhuri" trees began to murmur their tune greeting the birds in their nests. The chirping of the birds filled the air, welcoming the evening.

After a long exhausting day at work, Manjari started strumming her Sharod, sitting comfortably on a padded bench on her patio. She sat close to a tree with branches full of big red flowers. Growing upwards, they looked like the flames of a fire. Her long wavy black hair covered her arms.

The black clouds on the horizon appeared suddenly, and the wind came up, blowing Manjari's hair and exposing her sculpted arms. Her olive-colored skin looked brighter with the flash of lightning. Standing five foot three inches tall, Manjari's slim figure complimented her skin, her pointed nose and wide, black eyes that were melancholic. Her colorful sari, adorned with ostentatious jewelry, only enhanced her beauty. Manjari carried a mysterious air about her—not quite reserved, but guarded somehow. Only when someone was able to crack through her emotional shell was she able to show her relaxed nature.

Manjari lived in a small bungalow one hundred fifty kilometers from Kolkata, India. The year was 1972. She taught history at a nearby college in town. Her Sharod was the only precious possession she had saved from her past. The lightning and thunder continued to dominate the sky and with it Manjari's memories flashed. In her mind's eye, she could see the small village where she was born and where she had lived with her parents.

The village was on the other side of river Padma in the east side of undivided Bengal. Fond memories of her school and her friends passed by one by one like drifting clouds.

Lush green paddy fields and coconut trees bordered the village, and beyond that a railway threaded through the field. The trains whizzed by, whistling with the wind. A big pond occupied space near Manjari's home. It used to be full of clear blue water and blossoming pink lotuses during the autumn. This pond also supplied edible fish all year round.

The evenings, Manjari remembered, were spectacular—filled with clear starry skies, gentle breezes, chirping crickets, and dancing fireflies beyond the house around the paddy fields. As the evening drew its curtain, separating day from night, the frogs would begin their serenade and Manjari's eyelids would grow heavy until she fell asleep.

These were the days when people around the village exchanged niceties and seemed to trust each other. As the adults came home from a long day's work, children would settle in for the evening, busy preparing their homework for next day.

It was a very peaceful village existence that remained that way for many years.

Then one day in 1946, the life that young Manjari grew to love changed forever. An unrelenting, uneasy aura of secrecy that the nine-year-old didn't understand infiltrated the air.

One night Manjari's parents came and sat down next to her as she did her homework. Her mother, Bakul, fondly arranged her curly bangs as her father, Bipin, addressed her by her pet name.

"Manju we need to talk before you go to bed."

"Yes, daddy?"

"Manju, you probably noticed that some neighbors aren't so friendly anymore and have avoided us."

Manjari shrugged. "I noticed but don't know why. Did we do something wrong to make them angry?"

Her parents shook their heads sadly.

"You must know that there's religious unrest between Hindus and Muslims and it's escalating," Bipin said. "There was a time in this part of the country that there were temples and mosques around the villages and people practiced their own religious rites without question and celebrated each others' festivities. They are not happy right now with this arrangement and do not want to live peacefully, side by side together as we have done for so many years. The people are so angry at each other that they are destroying and looting things from the people who are not of the same religious belief as they are. Some groups are killing each other. The part of India where we are, and the extreme west side of India like Lahore and west side of Punjab, are very much affected."

"What are you talking about? People killing people of the same country? Does it mean that I am not going to be friends with Fatima and Sayeeda?"

"You will be always their friend," her father assured her. "All I'm saying is that if we have to risk our lives to live here then we have to move to a safer area, like a hundred kilometers away from the big city Kolkata. And I can take a teaching job there for the time being; until the situation improves."

"Mahjusona don't tell anyone, we have to leave our home secretly, so that no one knows," Bakul said. "Do you understand?"

Manjari felt confused and frightened. "No, I won't tell anyone. I promise."

Disillusioned by the way people were slaughtering each other, Manjari realized that one of her friends, Champa, had already left. It felt strange that Champa did not say goodbye to her. Champa's house and rice granary had been on fire. It was not an accident was it? Manjari realized that her father was right. Someone not to be trusted must have done harm to them.

The couple planned to leave their home with Manjari during a New Moon evening when an escape in the dark seemed more feasible. Then the day of their escape finally arrived; that ominous day when a peaceful evening settled with a hoot of an owl, soon interrupted by an unpleasant bang on the door followed by several loud voices coming from the front door.

"Who is it?" Bipin said. His voice dripped with fear.

Before he could open the door, the people stampeded their way through the door, dismantling and destroying the furniture and looting possessions on their destructive path.

Manjari, pale with fear and anxiety, ran to her mother Bakul and started sobbing. She grabbed her tightly with her two hands.

Bipin attempted to reason with the intruders whom he knew from school where he was the principal.

"Yusuf and Kareem you were my beloved students! What is wrong? Why are you doing this?"

"Why do you ask?" Yusuf snarled.

"You will find out soon."

Bipin and Yusuf wrestled. As Bipin tried to defend him, Kareem took out his sharp knife and plunged it into Bipin's chest who fell with a loud cry in a pool of his own blood.

"We have to transport these two to Mr. Khan's house," Kareem said. "Before that we can play around a little with these women. The girl is too young. We can wait till she matures."

Bakul, who heard the conversation, ran out to the kitchen only to succumb to the same sharp knife that took her husband's life. Soon Bipin and Bakul's blood combined into one large, tragic pool. Just a few feet away stood Manjari in shock from what she had witnessed.

"Please, let this just be a nightmare. Let it not be true," she pleaded silently.

Kareem pushed her down and tied her feet and both hands. They blindfolded her and threatened to torture her if she made noise. As they lifted her, she could imagine seeing her parents' pale faces for one last time. Even death couldn't erase a somewhat serene countenance as they passed from this dreadful world. She could remember the look on their faces as her kidnappers shoved her into a horse-drawn buggy that made a hasty escape. She could see the sky in her imagination as clear and starry as wind blew gently over her face. She truly believed that the fireflies danced madly around the paddy fields. Peace existed amid the smell of death.

Meanwhile, in NoyaKhali, the east part of Bengal, about twenty-five miles east of Manjari's tortured home, the scene at Mahatma Gandhi's Peace Camp was bustling as people occupied themselves with plans for a mission of liberation. Gandhi's followers fondly called him "Bapujee;" a name known by people all over India who regarded him as a father figure. Arun, who was a notable activist and instrumental in starting the camp, came forward and said, "Bapujee, Bivajee has arrived."

Arun had been arrested by the British government, as he was actively involved in the revolution against the British. He was imprisoned for four years. After he was released, he entered this part of the country disguised as a

Muslim orthodox cleric, as it was almost impossible to get in when the communal riot was at its peak. Arun was brave enough to start the peace camp alone to serve the distressed people who lost everything including loved ones in this sad, communal riot—and also to serve the children who lost their parents. After he established the peace camp, Mahatma Gandhi was notified, and he came to visit the camp himself and was pleased. It was in the news that "A peace camp exists in the east part of Bengal."

Biva, a recent graduate of Calcutta University, was a writer and vocalist in Indian classical music and took an active role with her physician husband in the underground work against British rule. She could not take the deception of living sheltered in the family when the rest of the country was in serious trouble.

Standing at five feet two inches tall, with a healthy smooth tanned complexion, Biva's triangular face held a prominent nose and beautiful wide, bright eyes, which sparkled. She tucked her long, wavy hair in a bun, which complimented her conservative attire. She was known to command an arresting presence everywhere she went.

The followers listened in awe as Gandhi discussed the various missions, many of them arduous and risky. He informed the camp that some girls had been kidnapped after their parents were murdered. For ten abducted girls people knew the places where they were taken. Negotiations would be offered for their freedom. But one girl, the daughter of a prominent school head master, whose whereabouts was unknown, captivated Biva's attention. She came forward and volunteered that she would take on the task of finding one of the missing girls; Manjari. Mahatma Gandhi expressed that the mission was risky but praised Biva for her bravery. After the discussion, Gandhi started his morning walk attired in his signature white outfit, firmly holding his long stick. With his followers in tow, they started singing a Tagore song loudly together:

> "If no one responds to your call, then you just march alone, on your own, on your own—keep going on your own. If no one shines light, Oh poor Hapless soul—If they shut the doors of their homes, on a dark tempestuous night, Then in the fire of lightning and thunder—Let the ribs of your chest be alight—And burn, burn alone!"

The peace march continued every morning for at least two hours. The march wound around the muddy unpaved road as their voices echoed through the swaying paddy fields and beyond. A train charged by at a distance beyond the tall coconut trees. The people around the villages anxiously looked through the window wondering what was going on.

"What is the purpose of this peace march?" some brave souls inquired.

"To let you know that we are here for you and with you. You are not alone," a peace marcher responded.

"Can you stop this? What role can we play in this mission?" a villager asked.

"I am not going to quit until I come to an agreement, and for you my advice would be to stand courageously together and confront the senseless communal riot between Hindus and Muslims," Gandhi replied.

After the peace march they came and began their sessions at a spinning wheel to spin yarn of their own to make their own clothes. Gandhi believed that if you could make your own yarn, and weave your own clothes, it would make you independent of buying clothes made in England.

The peace camp ran like a moderate-sized institution. There was a big kitchen where food was being prepared three times daily for distressed people who took shelter with the children, the children who had lost their parents and the people who were running the camp. A facility existed for the children to study and play and enjoy other activities to keep them busy. Gandhi made it clear that everything should be spotlessly clean around the camp and the adults who took refuge were given the responsibility all day long. There were two or three doctors on duty to deal with the ailments of the distressed people and children. At the end of the day there was a prayer meeting with devotional songs. One song said: "Almighty, please show us the path of peace, and bless us with the wisdom of peace. God or Almighty is the same one, with a different name Allah or Ishwar," and was followed by a discussion session. The day would end with the orange glow of the sun over the swaying paddy fields. The cool gentle breeze blew through the palm trees as the evening settled.

☙ ☙ ☙

Manjari was transported by horse-drawn buggy to Mr. Khan's place. Once they reached their destination, Manjari, still numb with shock, did not know where they had taken her. She looked around in the dark but could not see. The people who murdered her parents dragged her inside, and then she placed her weary head to rest on the floor. When she woke up she realized she must have been asleep for hours. Had the recent events been a nightmare? She realized the trauma actually happened. She tried to lift her head up, and saw some shadowy figure.

"Time to get up!" Manjari heard someone say.

Wearily she felt her cold feet and fingers tremble. She shuddered as she felt her nerves climb from her feet to her heart. Anxiety overcame her as a woman asked her name.

"Forget about that name," the woman curtly replied. "From now on you will be called Salatun."

Manjari kept quiet and did not want to confront her as she was actually overwhelmed by the fear of the unknown.

"Today I let you sleep late," the woman said. "Starting tomorrow you get up early and start your work of cleaning the entire house. You start cleaning downstairs, polish the furniture and Mashuma will let you know when you can go upstairs and start cleaning there. Mashuma is in charge of the kitchen where you're expected to help her. There are rules and regulations of the house, and you are going to listen to whatever she tells you to do. That is my order. Mashuma, show her where she will stay and give her some clothes and that black Borkha she'll always have to wear."

Mashuma seemed about her mother's age, Manjari thought. She was of average build and had wheat-colored skin. Her face was triangular with big black eyes that appeared kind. Mashuma's long black hair was pulled tightly in a bun. Over her white sari the black *burka* covered her body except her head and face.

"Salatun, please follow me," Mashuma softly uttered.

Manjari felt like crying out loud at the sound of her newly given name, but her throat was choking with fear and anxiety. She followed Mashuma to listen to the first of many orientations of this big mansion with many corridors and dark menacing corners. During this reluctant weary tour of the dungeon-like mansion, she realized how modest and tiny their cottage was, but it was nurtured with lots of love and affection. Looking back now, she knew that life with her parents could never be possible again.

Mashuma took Manjari to the end of the mansion and showed her the sleeping quarters. She told Manjari that the day started early—around five in the morning.

Then she went over a litany of arduous physically and mentally demanding household tasks such as cleaning all the rooms and corridors, both upstairs and downstairs, and tidying them up, and polishing the furniture. Manjari was forced to help prepare lunch and dinner. She was forbidden to go upstairs alone to clean the rooms and was always accompanied by Mashuma. As weary Manjari began to sob, Mashuma gave her a pat at the back and assured her she would help her.

Manjari toiled through the same routine orchestrated by the woman of the house and supervised by Mashuma. At times Manjari would encounter Sameema and her husband, Mr. Khan.

"Salatun, you did a sloppy job of tidying my bed," Sameema complained. "The bed spread should be changed every three days. I cannot stand to sleep in squalor and the mirror of my dresser has streaks. Next time I expect better than this."

It seemed to Manjari, that no matter how hard she tried, Sameema was never pleased.

So the unbearable days lingered on with only one relief—Mashuma's compassionate face and helping hand. At the risk of suffering from Sameema's wrath, Mashuma assisted in completing Manjari's household chores; including cleaning the obscenely large mirrors and dusting the framed photos of the Khan family. As she prepared the family's meals, Mashuma would encourage Manjari to take a break and engage her in conversation while still being on her guard, lest a family member barge in unexpectedly.

"This afternoon, the family will be gone to attend an event and are not expected to return till late evening," Mashuma said one day. "So I will take you out in the garden and we will chat to our heart's content. Finish the work quickly."

Manjari could not remember the last time she had been outdoors. Had it been months? A year?

While Manjari's heart was heavy with grief, the very idea of going outside made her eyes curious to see beyond the window. Manjari's mood briefly lifted as she stepped into the garden.

"I feel that I could breathe the fresh air, and I am so glad to smell the jasmine and tuberoses," Manjari said.

The gardenias were there in a medium-sized tree. She wanted to pluck one but, knowing that she was forbidden to do so, she avoided temptation to make contact with the flower.

Suddenly, memories of Manjari's once blissful home, with its pond and garden once lovingly tended by her mother, flooded her consciousness. She sunk her head and grieving heart and curled into a ball as she surrendered to tears. Mashuma came and patted her softly on the back.

Mashuma sighed as she shared her own tragic tale.

"You know Salatun I am also not Muslim, my name was changed, as these people would have killed us. In exchange, I begged them to save me and my husband's life, and I promised to serve them as long as they needed me."

Manjari waited until Mashuma continued her story.

"Our whole family—my parents and my child—planned to escape in two different delivery trucks of fruit and vegetables. But we got caught," Mashuma said.

"Do you know anything about your parents and daughter?" Manjari gently asked.

"Yes, that they are safe and alive residing at the outskirt of the big city Kolkata. But, my husband," Mashuma, paused, realizing she'd said too much. "That is all for today."

The black clouds gathered on the eastern side of the horizon as a blast of cool breeze blew through the trees. They heard a chorus of some sort that sounded like prayer songs from distance.

"That is from the Peace Camp of Mahatma Gandhi. It is on other side of the river," Mashuma told Manjari. "You see, the river is beyond that paddy field and the Peace Camp is farther away from the river bank. The Peace Camp is a place where the distressed people—victims of this senseless riot—can take refuge. I heard of it when we were planning to escape; it was the talk of the town and there were posters plastered in places like the vegetable and fish markets."

Manjari's memories of the last few days of peaceful existence with her parents came back to her. She remembered her father mentioning the name of Mahatma Gandhi and that Gandhi and his fellow volunteers had arrived about twenty-five miles from where they used to live. Manjari could hear the echo of his father's voice. It seemed so real to her: *You know the Peace Camp was started by a young spirited person recently released from prison. He was arrested for the activities of revolution against the British. There are two ladies involved also in this endeavor.*

Manjari remembered her father's words as tears rolled down her cheeks. She felt that the whole world was crashing in front of her, and she was just floating with her tied up hands and feet on an endless ocean of pain. She wished she could be at the Peace Camp now or join her parents in Heaven.

The weather changed abruptly, matching Manjari's mood, and it seemed that there was the possibility of rain, followed by lightning. The birds flew with agonizing chatter from one branch to other, warning each other of imminent danger.

Mashuma started collecting the mangoes, which the wind had blown from the trees, and started putting those in a basket. Then she and Manjari rushed back into the house.

If life was like the weather, Manjari thought, then she longed for the calm after the storm.

At Gandhi's Peace Camp, special events were shaping up. One of them was Biva's quest for Manjari.

"Why are you so eager to find this girl, Manjari?" one of the volunteers dared to ask Biva.

"Somebody has to take the risk of finding this girl," Biva boldly answered. "What happens if we abandon her? It would be cruel to not even try to save her."

Biva's grandmother once organized a protest with the women-folk to burn clothes made in England. As Indian-made clothes were banned, they had to suffer the wrath of the British Police and were arrested for civil disobedience. She also shared the stories of two young, educated women who risked their lives for the freedom of the country, and that she must have inherited her courage from her grandmother and father, both of whom served time in jail for fighting for freedom.

"Someone there who worked for the British authority planted a rifle in our backyard at night without our knowledge and accused my father of treachery," Biva explained passionately. "He was thrown in jail and tortured and all his hard-earned money as a school teacher was frozen by the British government to punish him. Fighting for freedom is in my blood. So I am determined to do my part to save this girl!"

At the Peace Camp, Arun, the director, strategized Biva's mission including choosing Dhiren, a guide familiar with the region, to accompany her. As the day of the rescue drew near, Biva focused on what lay ahead and, as possible obstacles invaded her thoughts, she tried to remain optimistic. Her worst fear was not finding Manjari. Biva thought about her husband's support, as he allowed her to pursue this important mission. Faces of her loved ones—her mother, father, grandmother, brothers and sisters—flashed in front of her as a sign that Biva had every reason to return home alive.

Then there was the plan to end one's life with respect—with honor and tradition—should the mission go awry.

Biva kept her cyanide package protected; nobody knew where she kept it. She planned to use it in a worst-case scenario, when she definitely would know that her honor was at stake. Arun knew her plan, so he instructed Dhiren to keep an eye on her as much as possible and under no circumstances was he to let her use the deadly poison as she might not be able to assess the situation and take the cyanide when it was not necessary. Arun gave this instruction to Dhiren: if he thought that Biva would be in real danger at the hand of the perpetrators and her honor would be at stake, Dhiren would behead Biva with a big sword and kill himself as well. Biva was not aware of this plan and neither was Gandhi. Gandhi expressed great concern over the mission to rescue Manjari, as this was the most dangerous mission of all.

Biva and Dhiren began their search for Manjari that day and continued for a week. The grueling search went on as they had to make up a different excuse each time to gain access inside homes when they visited local landlords. Sometimes they talked about the Peace Camp and invited them to visit Gandhi. Other times they discussed some road improvement project. They were getting frustrated with their search, as they didn't seem to be getting anywhere.

They were given the confidential information that a now ten-year-old abducted girl was held prisoner in a mansion of a rich landlord. So their target was to take a chance to investigate a few more rich landlords' mansions on the other side of river.

So the search for Manjari continued. The evening was peaceful and spectacular. The sky greeted them with stars, while the earth gifted them with a gentle breeze and wild fireflies.

From one side of the river stretched a unique bridge consisting of two bamboo planks, which lay horizontally side by side and tied together. The end of either side was fortified with strong vertical bamboo poles. As Biva clutched a covered lantern close to her body, she found that crossing the river in pitch darkness became a real gymnastic maneuver, so Biva advised her attendant to swim and wait for her on the other side of river.

When she arrived at the gate of the huge mansion she told the gatekeeper that she wanted to talk to the lady of the house. The gatekeeper was hesitant, but with Biva's persistent request, he finally granted her permission. Samema, accompanied by Mashuma, greeted Biva, who explained that she and her other companions were touring this area to see if anyone was interested in volunteering their time to help build roads or help get electricity and safe, accessible drinking water.

"Are you interested in becoming involved in this project?' Biva asked.

Samema seemed honored as she was never asked and given a chance to take an important role outside her household, so she invited the guests inside the house. Mashuma suddenly excused herself saying she wanted to check on something. In the meantime, Sameema left to find her attendant to make some tea and snacks.

At that very moment Manjari appeared to dust the photos and rosewood chairs in the long corridor. She was curious about the visitors and hoped they would notice her presence.

Biva's radar targeted the young girl immediately. It was Manjari.

"Did someone bring you here?" Biva whispered as she grabbed the girl's hand. "Manjari? Is it you?"

Manjari suppressed a sob as she heard her name.

"I've come to rescue you," Biva whispered.

"But, I do not know you," Manjari protested. "Are you really going to help?"

"There is no time to discuss," Biva replied anxiously. "You must trust me. There is no other way for you to get out from this place. Show me a window or open space from where we can try to get out."

With a strong sense she could trust this woman, Manjari quickly guided Biva to a small bathroom with an open window. They had to step onto a toilet to climb out of the room. Then, after Biva jumped out, she urged Manjari to jump into her arms.

"Don't worry. I'll catch you," Biva assured her. "You can trust me."

Manjari closed her eyes. This was it. Her ticket to freedom. She would risk escaping with this stranger or stay and die. Manjari surrendered into Biva's waiting arms. Relief soared through both their hearts. But they both ran as fast as they could. It was too early to celebrate. They had to run for their lives.

Covered with the same black *burka* Manjari wore, they blended into the darkness. Biva knew they needed to reach the bank of the river soon, but the shrubs and darkness made the path almost unbearable. They heard some noise and could see some semblance of roving lights near the mansion from a distance. They hurried their pace, tripping over branches, as they knew pursuers were on their way. At last they reached the bank of the river where Biva's attendant Dhiren was waiting. He helped them descend into the river and told them to swim under the water as long as they could and momentarily lift their heads up to catch their breaths. Every moment was filled with uncertainty as they swam in the darkness. Manjari was glad that her father had taught her one of the greatest gifts of life—how to swim. Now, she wasn't just swimming to save her life. She was swimming to honor her parents.

They swam to the safe side of the river and finally reached the shore of the Peace Camp. As they reached the camp, the guard dogs started barking with excitement. The Peace Camp was barbed-wired all around, and there were armed guards with swords and bamboos. Guards posted themselves at each of the four corners of the camp.

They were specially trained to defend and fight in any emergency, and Arun demanded that the guards serve vigilant eight-hour shifts. Suddenly, the Peace Camp erupted into peals of relief and jubilation as they greeted the long-awaited arrivals, who were laden with mud and exhaustion but lucky to be alive.

The next few surreal hours passed as Manjari realized that she was no longer in danger. On the way to the Peace Camp, they heard the continuous serenade of crickets and croaking of frogs. Their vision turned over the paddy fields where the fireflies were dancing madly. Freedom was hers.

Manjari couldn't sleep that night. She kept thinking this was all a dream—that she was really still back at the mansion with that horrible Sameema's barking orders. Then gradually, she absorbed the ambience of the place her father mentioned at a time that seemed like ages ago. There were other young children in the camp, a few accompanied by their parents, while others lost their fathers, and some were totally orphaned like her. Day after day, she adjusted to life at the camp. Manjari continued to trust Biva—after all, the woman risked her own life to save hers. Trust turned into gratitude and gratitude turned into love. What choice did Manjari have but to choose love—which always conquered fear, her mother had told her. In time, Biva would become a surrogate mother to Manjari.

Then one day, Manjari received an unforgettable invitation—a chance to meet Gandhi.

"He is very kind and he loves all the children very much," Biva assured her.

When Mahatma Gandhi arrived, everyone in the camp seemed to be in collective awe in his presence. The children gathered round, waiting to be hugged by the great leader as though he was their grandfather—the Father of all Fathers.

"I prayed for my Dad," said one little boy whose father was murdered.

"I pray for your long healthy and happy life," Gandhi told the boy.

Biva introduced Manjari to Gandhi who seemed very pleased to see them.

"With God's grace I am happy to see you alive and healthy," he said. "Biva, I am so happy to see you, and I am very proud that you fulfilled your task with courage and determination."

He turned to Manjari. "Manjari, my child, come here. Biva risked her life to save you. Always know that your parents are in a more peaceful place, and they are constantly watching over you."

Manjari was in tears as she hugged Biva. This was the first time she showed her intense emotion to Biva. Gandhijee ushered Biva and Manjari to a room where a mat made of knitted palm leaves was spread across the floor. There were a few pillows with embroidered covers laid on the mat at the corner, and a large clay vase with tuberoses. A large spinning wheel sat in the middle of room waiting to be spun.

"I heard you did very well in school," Gandhi told Manjari. "Do you want to continue your studies?"

"How? My parents are no more," Manjari wondered as tears began to well in her eyes.

"We know your situation," Gandhi said. "Suppose we arranged for it?"

Manjari expressed her concern over not knowing where she would live. Gandhi assured her that volunteers had raised funds to open a new school with a dormitory for the girls set to open soon around the city of Kolkata.

"You will go there and continue your education," he said. "You have to do it for yourself and for your parents to survive in this world. Biva will look after you and guide you when ever you need her."

Manjari was overwhelmed with joy and simultaneous fear of the unknown. Despite her tears Manjari raised a smile of gratitude to Biva, who returned her smile. In the background, the singing vibrated all over Peace Camp. They were singing:

> "If everyone goes back / Oh you poor
> hapless soul / While you walk on the
> desolate road, no one looks back / Then just
> move on, trampling the thorns on the road
> under your bloodied feet. / All on your own."

India got independence and the country was divided. Manjari attended boarding school with Biva as a mentor. She gradually overcame her emotional hurdles that outweighed her academic challenge. She slowly learned to adjust and regain control over her traumas with Biva's guidance and support as the years went by. Even as Biva had children of her own, she was always there to see Manjari achieve important personal and educational goals.

Years later, as head of the history department in a university college one hundred and fifty kilometers from Kolkata, Manjari thought about how to make history come alive to her students. She smiled peacefully as she decided she would share with her students and with future generations, her own tale, her parent's tale and her country's story of love, pain, survival and freedom.

As the evening settled in slowly, the smell of the exotic "Mohua" flower wafted through the air just as the red moon peeped through the distant mountain range. Manjari could hear the beating of "Madal" percussion drum as the tribes danced and sang along with the gentle breeze. Manjari closed her eyes as she embraced the memories—both good and bad—of her village, parents, her slavery in that mansion, Biva, and the Peace Camp. The song rang eternally in her head: "If all of them turn their faces, feeling scared / One and all, then just open your heart . . . This is the ballad of peace, love and freedom for all."

Douglas Burgess

Douglas Burgess is a retired Art Director who spent nearly forty-five years in advertising departments at companies such as Safeway, Pacific Stereo, CBS, and Rhone-Poulenc.

He earned his B.F.A. degree from the California College of the Arts and completed his graduate work in Graphic Design at U.C. Berkeley.

Since suffering a stroke in 2011, Douglas has been a resident of Grace Healthcare of Pleasant Hill, California, where he is Resident Council President.

His written work is primarily memoir filled with details about his very interesting and sometimes astounding life as an army brat.

Standin' at the Crossroads

Unfortunately, I had to work overtime that evening, so as I approached the club I could hear the din of the opening act a block away. T-Bone Carter and the Bluesbusters were playing their rendition of *Little Red Rooster*, the Howling Wolf Classic.

T-Bone had worked with The Wolf and Robert Johnson in the Delta before they moved north to Chicago to play on the "chitlin circuit" in those legendary clubs on the South Side. That gravel-pit voice of the Wolf had been silenced a few months before and T. Bone was the bluesman to have the closest bite or hard edge sound of the original.

I had seen Muddy Waters in his last Bay Area performance a month prior to this and he looked like he had been literally propped up and was just going through the motions of playing his guitar. Thankfully, Pinetop Perkins was in rare form and carried the show as the band rocked on and he played his boogie-woogie blues. A month later, Muddy left us for good.

Tonight, T-Bone was doing a tribute to the Wolf, Muddy, and Robert Johnson. T-Bone was always unpretentious and totally down to earth, with such titles as *Cockroach, The Sky is Crying, Crosscut Saw,* and the showpiece, *Standin' at the Crossroads*. His band was featured tonight along with a small local band that was the opening act. They tried to reach the lofty heights of T-Bone's group, but like Icarus, suffered a meltdown.

Never mind, I was now safely in my seat on the balcony with no one in front of me, just the railing. The opening act was concluding their set and T-Bone's band was hovering in the wings. Soon they came out and started their intro, a fine version of *Kansas City*. As the number ended the drum roll announced that The Man himself was here.

"Let's have a big San Francisco welcome for the real King of Blues . . . his honor, Mr. T-Bone!"

In a sequin cape and sequin dark glasses, The Man himself strode out on the stage and immediately started playing his steel guitar. He called it finger-lickin'-pickin' and it was. The base pounded so hard you thought your heart might explode any minute. The bass started barking on each guitar break. The piano chimed in and soon that unmistakable voice came out of the mike and enveloped the room. "The sky is cryin' . . . look at the tears roll down the street" . . . it was so-o-o good!

As the music got louder the balcony began to palpitate. Did anyone worry that it might just collapse from the vibrations? Hell no, everyone started tapping their feet and clapping their hands. The solo guitar cut like a sabre through the air never missing a beat. It began to have a voice of its own, whining one minute, squealing with pleasure the next. Then getting down to the lower registers it went back to its plaintive blues asking . . . "Why, Baby, Why?"

T-Bone had finished his first set and it was time for me to go backstage and visit The Man himself. I had a personal invitation as I had played a gig or two with him in my younger days when I played in my high school band. Back then I played a flute, though my real love was the harmonica . . . the blues harmonica to be precise. As a teenager I used to listen to the local black rhythm and blues station, which featured many Bay Area blues artists as DJs. That's where I first heard T-Bone. I actually called him up to request one of his numbers and he was very friendly. He said, "Do you play gigs?"

I said, "No, just the flute in the high school band . . . but I really love the blues harmonica!"

"You know Little Milton?"

"Sure do . . . he's my favorite harmonica man," I said emphatically. T-Bone then invited me over to his place and asked me to bring my harmonica.

When I first saw him I found him sitting in the living room of an old run-down Victorian in a very battered wicker chair. It was his favorite chair. It almost looked like a porcupine as it was full of splinters and although duct tape had not been invented then, there were scraps of electrical and masking tape around worn joints. As he sat in it and rocked it sounded like an old clipper ship in a Nor'easter, creaking and yawing in the wind. As he rocked in a slower, steadier pace, you could feel the sea calm as though the clipper were sailing out of the storm, steady as she goes. He would then have a contented look on his face like a skipper who had survived the wrath of a typhoon and was heading to his ports of call on time and on course.

He pulled out one of his Prince Edward cigars. In a long, leisurely sort of way, he struck the match on the side of the box, dragging it like a piece of chalk across a blackboard so that it had a slow screech until the tip of the match sparked and the flame burst forth like a Fourth of July firecracker. He took a couple of puffs to make sure the stogie was lit, as he settled into the wicker chair as if he were camping out for the night.

"Well, Bub," a nickname he soon gave me, which he called his grandkids, "let's see what you got on that harmonica of yours."

He then pulled his worn-out bottleneck guitar that had traveled up from the Delta to Chicago, to New York, to New Orleans, and on to 'Frisco. It was called Cindy Lou as in "Can you be true, Cindy Lou."

"Do you know Elmore James . . . *The Sky is Crying?*"

"Sure do," I said.

"Let's go to it then!" His fingers started picking the long intro before the lyrics entered in a wailing melancholy way . . . "Oh, the sky is cryin' . . . look at the tears roll down the street." And before the bottleneck guitar could assert itself again, I cut in with the harmonica trying to keep up with T-Bone as he started picking the bottleneck with renewed ferocity.

"Sounds real good, Bub—you're a natural man."

I blew harder till you thought I was a steam engine going down the tracks at full throttle.

"That's it, son, give it all you got . . . you're a rambling man, a hobo on the freight train of life. Let me feel that lonely feelin'."

I started going downscale to give it a sad, plaintive note, and then I built up to a crescendo that would blow the roof off the house.

"That's it! Now ya got it, Bub." We were rockin and we knew it. "No better feelin' than dat, Man," T-Bone kept shouting.

We ended our jamming and he said, "Why don't you join my band next Saturday night as my guest at Ruthy's Inn, okay?"

I was thrilled. "I'll be there!" I said, almost without realizing it.

"First, though, you gotta come to rehearsal with the band on Friday night and it'll be a long, late run as we jam into the wee hours of the morning in order to get da spirit down . . . can ya dig it man?"

"Yep, I sure can. When do you want me to show?"

"Make it about eight, man, 'cause we don't start really rockin' till midnight."

"Gotcha," I said.

I got there at 7:30 and after a proper intro to the band members, we started getting down to da blues. There was Pinetop Perkins on the ivories, a young Buddy Guy on guitar, Ray 'Mad Dog' Nitscke on percussion, Freddy King on base—all the best bluesmen of the time.

"Let's do *Standin' at the Crossroads*," T-Bone shouted out. "It's the classic Robert Johnson song about selling his soul to the Devil in order to be the best bluesman there ever was, "standin' at the crossroads of good and evil, of fame and shame, rags or riches . . . you make the choice." But it was more than that; it was about risking everything to be the best.

"What will you do when you're standin' at the crossroads? Play it like you mean it!" T-Bone shouted. "Da devil's lookin' you in da eye . . . whatcha gonna do?"

Pinetop started it out pounding the keyboards in the New Orleans barrelhouse blues style as Freddie thumped the bass so that it started pumpin' like a heart on speed. "Mad Dog" picked up with the percussion and Buddy got into it with his guitar. Then it was my turn to start wailin' on my harmonica before T-Bone started singing the lyrics. I was out of sync with the band and T-Bone sensed that I was nervous performing for the first time with these legendary musicians. He shouted, "Hold on, Bub, let's go over this lick . . . let's get it like we did it at my place."

He asked for my harmonica and started right in with the greatest sound I had ever heard from that instrument. He made it sound like a cathedral pipe organ, like Bach had composed a blues cantata. The sounds emanated from all sides, up and down the scale, and back again, a band in itself. It was then that I really knew that the blues were every bit as classical as the Philharmonic and that T-Bone was Toscanini.

T-Bone said, "When I came up North from Dixie I brought da sound wit me . . . Bub, do you know what sound dat was?"

"The sound of Robert Johnson at the crossroads!"

"You got it, Bub, but what *is* that sound*?*"

"I'm not sure."

"Well, what is the crossroads of Highway 61 and Highway 49?"

"It's North/South, right?"

"One goes to Chicago, the other to the Delta."

"What's the difference?"

"The Delta's the old rural blues. Chicago's the electrified urban blues."

"Right on!" T-Bone responded. "So yous is standin' at the crossroads of what?"

"You mean like the old versus the new, freedom versus oppression, progress versus the past?"

"You got it, Bub. Robert Johnson had mastered the Delta blues. There was nothing left for him to do down south. He needed to leave his past behind and take his message North. He needed to leave the lynchin', the cross burnin', the back of the bus, the separate drinkin' fountains."

"You mean he needed an electric sound—to match the factory workers that headed north and suffered other but different forms of discrimination?"

"The blues needed a new sound, a sound of machinery, a beat of clanking and clinking, of metal against metal, of electrical fireworks, of echoes of syncopation."

"Did he sell his soul to the devil to do this?" I asked naively.

"No, but he cut a deal with him just the same."

"How's that?" I asked.

"He asked the devil to give him a new, unforgettable sound that would make Robert a legend and then he asked the devil what he wanted in return. Well, the devil then appeared before him as the Grand Dragon of the Ku Klux Klan and along with the largest cross he ever saw burnin' behind him was the biggest Stars and Bars flag a-flutterin' in da wind. The devil nodded to him and pointed North to Highway 61 and said, *Boy, you must promise me you'll head North and never come back to Dixie again because we're tired of niggers bitchin' about their condition South of the Mason-Dixon Line. Can you do dat?*"

"Robert smiled and said, "*Sho nuff!*"

"*Well,* the Grand Dragon said, *this deal is done. Now get your black ass out of Dixie and don't never return.*"

"Robert was thumbin' a ride and soon a Model-T with Illinois plates appeared. It stopped and Robert asked the driver where he was headed. The man said, *I'm headed home to Chicago.*"

"Robert replied, *Me too,* having never been there in his life. Now Robert had beat the devil at his own game. The blues headed North, East, and West from the U.S.A. to Europe to Asia to Africa and right back to the Delta itself."

T-Bone struck a wide grin and started laughing as he said, "Dat Devil Klansman was sure snookered, 'cause now when you mention da Delta, you think of the blues and you think about Robert Johnson. Now, Bub, let's play it like you yourself are standin' at the crossroads . . ."

Later when we did our gig I just kept thinkin' about Highway 61 and Robert Johnson and the music flowed as the crowd cheered!

Bugle Calls

❦

Fort Meyers, Virginia is situated right across the
Potomac River from Washington D.C. There are two
Army posts there known as the North Post and the South
Post.

In between the two posts lies Arlington National
Cemetery, the official resting place of the Unknown
Soldier on grounds that had belonged to Robert E. Lee.
At the highest point in the cemetery lies the Lee Mansion,
which was founded by Robert E. Lee's grandfather, the
illustrious Revolutionary War hero Harry Lighthorse Lee.
Most of the men buried there were victims of the Army
of Northern Virginia commanded by Robert E. Lee.
These brave men were members of the Army of the
Potomac first commanded by McClellan, then Meade, and
finally Ullyses S. Grant whose initials were said to
represent his only terms: that is "Unconditional
Surrender" Grant.

As a young teenage Army Brat I had become
fascinated with all the battlefields of the Civil War that
surrounded Washington D.C. I used to go on expeditions
in search of the past and tried to relive the plight of my
ancestors who had fought in the Iron Brigade from
Lookout Mountain to Atlanta. I could envision Custer
fording the river and telling McClellan it was alright for
the troops to cross here. I could hear the caissons rolling

across the makeshift bridges, the men yelling at the mules to get a move on. I could hear the crack of the Springfields' volleys. I could hear the drum and bugle corps playing Yankee Doodle, the only song that Grant ever acknowledged knowing, saying he could never remember the words. Grant used this ploy in getting out of going to Ford's Theater that fateful night, telling Lincoln he was no devotee to music or drama.

Yet, there was more. There was a dream I had one special evening that began with the sound of Taps when the sun had set and all military personnel were required to bed down for the night. As I lay down to sleep, I could hear the fading echoes of the bugle pass over the tombstones of these fallen comrades as if kissing each one goodnight. Was it in remembrance of the last caress of a mother for her son, a wife for her husband, or a sister for her brother? A thousand bugles could not recreate the cries of the wounded at Shiloh, Antietam, Spotsylvania, or Gettysburg.

How practical they were to put nametags on each other, before battle, so their bodies could be identified amongst tomorrow's dead. With dire humor I could hear Jones tell Jim . . . "Well, buddy, I made the letters big enough so the sharpshooter can dot the 'I'." Jim would then say, "I will make your 'o' look like a bull's-eye." Then they would both laugh and say, "It's time to get some shuteye."

It was in this way that I would start to doze off to sleep and my dream would begin. From out of the darkness of the cemetery there was a distant flicker of light from torches on the march coming ever closer. The sound of regimental band music could be heard. The tramping of feet marching in unison was distinct. Soon the colors of different units emerged. The real astounding thing was this: These brigades were not just Civil War units. Here, in all their glory, was every famous band of troops from the Rough Riders to the Rainbow Division—yes, even the Iron Brigade.

As the battle flags unfurled and all the soldiers passed in review they were heading for some bivouac in order to assemble so they might camp. It was here that they would spend the night telling each other their stories of derring do and bravery, of camaraderie; but never of death or dying or of pain or of loss. This was their celebration to honor one another. Of finding buddies they thought were lost but now were found. It was the universal reunion of all veterans from every war telling their stories.

As MacArthur said . . . "Old soldiers never die . . . they just fade away." And there, in my dream, there he was himself—MacArthur—puffing on his corncob pipe, wearing his Colonel's uniform from his World War I Rainbow Division, his favorite, the one that made his career. Suddenly, he turned to me and said, "Your name is Douglas too." Flabbergasted I said, "Yes . . . in fact I am named after you."

"Good boy," he said. "Let's sit by the campfire and hear these stories." To my surprise there stood General

Patton with his pearl-handled revolvers. "Best damn men I've seen. Old Black Jack would be proud, don't ya think, Mac?" MacArthur winked in acknowledgement.

"But have you seen Andy Jackson's Kentucky Long Rifles?"

"You're right, Mac, he's one helluva man . . . I loved it when he whipped old Monty's ancestors real bad." As Patton and Mac were talking, I slipped away to join some of the regular foot soldiers that were starting to mill around and set-up their own individual campfires.

"Hey, boy come on over here," I heard a voice say. In the flicker of the firelight I could see a bearded man wearing the badge of the 3rd Michigan, a part of the Iron Brigade. He said, "Are ya one of those drummer boys I saw at Gettysburg?"

"No," I said. "I am just on a field trip to take notes for a school report."

"A student are ye now, eh?" he said. "What's your name?" he asked.

"Douglas . . . Douglas Burgess . . . ," I said.

"Well, what a coincidence! That's my last name too!"

"Were you at Lookout Mountain?" I asked.

"Sure was . . . all the way to Atlanta with Sherman to the sea. In fact, I was the guy who brought that complainin' Rebel plantation owner to Sherman when he protested the troops had taken everything he had."

Old General Sherman wasn't spooked as he looked down at the man who was riding a mule instead of a horse. With a mean look and a chaw of tobacco, he spit it out in front of the man as he looked him straight in the eye. "Couldn't have been my men, otherwise you wouldn't have that mule." With that old Tecumseh wheeled his mount around and rode off. "What a man he was . . . even Grant couldn't hold a candle to him."

We sat around the campfire and I asked as many questions as I could about the march South. "Sergeant Sam" as he was known, told me about the miracle of Missionary Ridge, how all the men in unison launched an impossible attack uphill and scared the Rebs right off the ridge, the attack being so fast that the Reb General Buckner was captured before he could sound retreat.

"What a day that was! Grant and Sherman had watched from below with their telescopes as the troops launched the attack on their own without having been given orders to do so. Of course, because it was so successful they were not reprimanded but became heroes because of their *esprit-de-corps!*"

"Wow," I said. "I've read all about that." Showing off my Civil War knowledge, I asked, "What about the reprimand General Thomas got from Grant for chewing out a Private in review for not having his belt buckle polished and thereby holding up the attack?"

"Yep, I was there. It was old private Johnson, old because he had been a Sergeant and served before the war, but he hit the bottle a little too often and he was stripped of his stripes. He was slow gettin' up that morning and just made it in line when General Thomas inspected the troops. Thomas looked down and said, 'Soldier, what's that grit on your belt buckle?' Private Johnson just said 'Sorry, Sir!' The General said, "Get back to your tent and spit and polish that buckle so the next time I see it I'll get a blind spot in my eye from the reflection."

"Yes, sir!" he replied. We all stood at attention until Private Johnson returned to ranks. The General bent down to take a closer look at the buckle when a messenger came from General Grant. Thomas squinted at the message, spit on the ground, and said, "Boys, let's get movin' so we can whip those Rebs!" Grant's message had read:

> *General, where the hell are your men? The attack*
> *was to commence at 0600 hours and it's past 0630.*
> *Did you misunderstand your order? Send a*
> *messenger to me at once saying your men are on the*
> *move lest I send a Brigadier General out to relieve*
> *you of your command.*
> *Sincerely,*
> *U.S. Grant.*

General Thomas was known as the 'Rock of Chicamagua' for his famous stand at that battle. He had a reputation to protect and he knew Grant meant business. He never had inspections before a battle after that.

As Sam was speaking, I began to hear the familiar Reveille from the bugler announcing it was morning and time for the men to move on. I had noticed nobody had slept the whole night through. I said, "Sam, it's morning already and the troops are assembling to move on without having bedded down for the night!"

"Yes, son," he said. "We sleep during the day now and stay up all night. The night belongs to the dead who must search for missing friends and family. The day belongs to the living whose purpose is to perpetuate friends and family. It's your job to continue the legacy we have given you at such great sacrifice."

At that point I heard Reveille from the bugler in Arlington National Cemetery near the tomb of the Unknown Soldier and I woke up, hearing my father shuffling around in the bathroom. He came into my room and said, "Son, it's 6:00 a.m. and time to get a move on."

I said, "Yes, Sir." I made sure my belt buckle sparkled as I left the house to get on the Army bus to take me to school.

Camaraderie
From: *Army Brat Stories*

❧

I was a curiosity, the only American enrolled in school, but I soon realized the other students had this image that I was some Hollywood figure.

I had just turned ten years old and was living in London. Since there were no American schools set up for U. S. military personnel, I had been going to Marleybone, an English school located not too far from Madame Tussaud's Wax Museum. I wore a typical English schoolboy's outfit of a cap, shirt and tie with blazer, short pants and knee socks. I was a Brit in every way. Until I opened my mouth that is . . . then I was a Yank!

They thought all Americans were glamorous Hollywood star material. Of course, it didn't help that every day a chauffeur brought me to school in a Rolls Royce. My father served as an attaché to the U.S. Embassy, so I got special treatment. In reality, I just felt happy that they accepted me and enjoyed my fellowship. I used to pull stunts like singing the lyrics to *America* instead of *God Save the King*. It was all in good fun.

However, one day a serious incident came my way. It involved the cracking and eating of coconuts on campus. This was an absolute no-no. (Eating on school grounds that is . . . nothing against coconuts.) The Headmistress caught me and a few of my chums red handed. She could have been a cameo of Queen Victoria.

92

She was dead serious, not a funny bone in her body. She took us straight to the Headmaster for a serious discussion about following rules and regulations.

The Headmaster was standing in front of a portrait of the Prime Minister, who had attended the school many years before. Suddenly, he turned while pointing directly at the portrait and fixed his gaze on us. In a terse deadly serious voice he exclaimed, "Do you think HE would choose to eat coconuts on the premises? Never . . . Never . . . Never!" he said while glancing at the Headmistress, who nodded in agreement.

With a glare towards us he asked, "What kind of punishment would he demand?" We huddled together and spoke not a word. Fear had gripped us and our expressions said it all. He turned to face the portrait and spoke with his back to us.

"Tomorrow before the assembled students you will extend each of your hands and be struck three times with the rod." We shuddered at this pronouncement not so much because of the pain that would be inflicted by the rod, but at the public humiliation.

As we were being escorted out the door by the Headmistress, the Headmaster beckoned to me. I hesitated and turned to see what he had to say to me. The other boys were whisked away, but not before they heard the Headmaster say that since I was an American and maybe not familiar with the British ways, I would not have to suffer this punishment with the other boys.

Somewhere deep inside of me welled up a singular disgust at this opportunity to be left off the hook, to be denied the camaraderie that I had developed with these boys who were to be punished for what I myself had also indulged in. In a firm reply that even surprised me I said, "I cannot accept!"

Without flinching, the Headmaster said, "Very well then. The punishment will be carried out tomorrow! Be off with you!"

The next day came all too fast and I was determined not to flinch. We assembled in the great hall to sing *God Save The King* before the beginning of our classes. I was with my chums, who had said nothing to me as they figured I had cut my deal with the Headmaster. I said nothing to them either as I did not want to let them know what I had done. The anthem ended and it was our turn for the rod.

The Headmaster stood up and announced that he wanted the students' attention as there was going to be a public punishment of some rascals who had intentionally broken school rules. These rascals were to be struck three times on each hand with the rod. The crime was eating coconuts on school grounds!

"But let me make this perfectly clear," he said. "The real crime is not following the rules that have been established here for generations." Scowling into the mass of students he exclaimed, "Would these boys have done their duty for Nelson at Trafalger? Would they have been one of the boys at Eton who won the Battle of Waterloo for Wellington? I daresay NOT! We cannot allow such diversions as the eating of coconuts on school grounds to distract us from our calling of developing the brightest and the best for King and Country. The Empire expects only sterling performances on our part and we must deliver!" Suddenly, he turned in my direction and called my name. "Master Burgess! Approach the platform!"

My chums gave a start and pushed one another and then gave me a quick shove onto the platform. I knew then I had gotten back in their good graces. I knew that I was following the rules of King and Country and I had done the right thing by taking my punishment. I extended my hand and invited the Headmaster to give it his best shot.

First one whack . . . then two whacks . . . and finally, the third. I did not flinch. I just kept looking at my chums who were smiling. It was the smile of buddies who from time immemorial created bonds of blood under tree houses, and in school playgrounds. The mission was trust, as solid as any handshake. There is no litigation amongst chums.

Each of us took our turn. Each of us took our bruises. Each of us knew it had nothing whatsoever to do with eating coconuts on school grounds!

The General

From: Army Brat Stories

◆

In 1953, I was eleven years old. My father was
stationed in Frankfurt, Germany as part of the Army of
Occupation. We lived in quarters on the outskirts of town
in a village called Hedernheim on Heidenfeld Street.

One day I accompanied my father to the General
Headquarters in downtown Frankfurt for a staff meeting,
waiting for him in an adjacent lounge area. As I was just
reading some magazines and trying to keep myself
occupied until the meeting was over, I noticed the
elevator door open. Out stepped a Four-Star General with
all sorts of commendation ribbons on his chest. Even
then I could recognize the Silver Star, The Legion of
Merit, Purple Heart, and medals showing he had served in
the major theaters of war, including North Africa, Sicily,
Italy, France, Belgium and Germany.

He walked with a swagger that said, "I don't need
no stinkin' swagger stick." I knew Patton was dead, but
who was this general that seemed to copy his every move.
To my horror, he looked at me and proceeded in my
direction. He bent over and looked me square in the eye
and said, "Son, I have a question for you." As was the
custom in the military I said firmly, "Yes, Sir!" (It didn't
need to be a General for you to say "Yes, Sir!" Every male
adult was addressed that way. You always said it with

emphasis, with a huge exclamation point. "Esprit de Corps!" my father would say. "You must always show Esprit de Corps!")

The General continued, "You see that sign out there on the way out of headquarters?"

"Yes, Sir!"

"What does it say, son?"

"Sir, it says Munich sixty km, Heidelberg one hundred and twenty km, Wiesbaden seventy-five km."

"Well, son, what does the 'km' stand for?"

"Sir," I said, "I don't know exactly."

The General moved closer to me, almost in my face, and said, "I am going to give you one big hint."

"Yes, Sir!" I said with emphasis.

"What do Germans eat a lot of, son?"

I had to think fast and I replied, "Frankfurters, Sir!"

He said, "Close but no cigar. What do they usually eat with those frankfurters and for accuracy's sake we will call them Bratwurst."

Again, I thought hard. "Sir! Sauerkraut, Sir!"

"Bingo!" he said. "You may be West Point material after all. Now do you get it, son?"

"Sir, it means you have to drive seventy kilometers to get some good Bratwurst and Sauerkraut?"

"No, son, no. It means Munich is sixty kraut miles away, Heidelberg's one-hundred-and-twenty and Wiesbaden is seventy-five. That's what Patton and I always said km stood for: Kraut Miles. Got it?" He patted me on the back and left with a belly laugh that could have been heard two hundred Kraut miles away. As he marched out the door he gave me a wink and saluted. I saluted back with vigor!

Soon, my father emerged from the meeting and said, "Did you see General McAuliffe as he left the building?"

"Yes, I think so, Sir."

"Do you know who he is?"

"No, Sir, but he said he served with Patton, Sir!"

My father said, "He's the General that said, 'Nuts to the Germans' when they asked him to surrender at Bastogne in the Battle of the Bulge. It was the best answer he could have given because it took the Germans so long to translate his reply that it allowed Patton to relieve his encircled Division. The Germans didn't know if it meant 'yes' or 'no', and they held back their attack until it was confirmed. By then it was too late and the opportunity of the cloud cover that had protected German troops had disappeared and our Air Force could strike at will against the Germans whose forces were now all exposed."

"Wow! I knew he was a war hero and to think he spoke to me!"

"Good work, son, he wouldn't have talked to you very long if you hadn't held up your end of the conversation."

"Yes, Sir," I said with complete satisfaction. I never ate sauerkraut again without thinking of my conversation with General McAuliffe.

The Pocket Knife
From: *Army Brat Stories*

◆

Rummaging through the drawer of my roll-top desk, I came across my first pocketknife.

It was an old mother-of-pearl handle model with only three blades, the longest blade being perhaps three inches in length. The little metal designs on the grip had been worn so smoothly into the mother-of-pearl handle it was as though it had been poured like molten steel onto the grip. The dust that had accumulated between the blades appeared as cobwebs within the grooves.

As I picked it up and examined it more closely, I could see my reflection in the worn metal plate, but it was not that of the child who had received it so many years before. The gray beard blended into the silver plate as in one of those last self-portraits of Rembrandt . . . you know, the ones that stare out from the canvas piercing the soul of every individual that dares to look back at it, yet asking through the pigment those eternal questions about the meaning of life and death, struggle and endurance.

Suddenly, I could see twelve-year-old Janet's steel blue eyes looking down on me while her curly black hair swirled in the wind coming off the beach of the White Cliffs of Dover. Her younger sister Pat came running up and screamed, "We've got Master Douggie now," as she scooped up some sand and playfully threw it at me. The two girls squealed with delight as they ruffled my hair and poured seawater over my head.

Janet whispered something to her sister and Pat disappeared. Janet ruffled my hair some more and looked me square in the eye. Without hesitation she asked, "Would you like to kiss me?" Startled, I asked, "Why?"

She gave me a look of disdain and said, "Because I want you to! If you're afraid or shy, let's go behind the rocks on the beach and do it."

"No," I said, "I don't want to!"

She took me by the hand anyway and moved towards the rock . . . I followed without resistance, but was still annoyed.

"Here," she said, "Let's do it!"

I resisted, but she was determined. She grabbed me and kissed me on the lips. My initial reaction was to push her off. She lost her balance, fell, and scraped her arm upon the rocks. The tissue broke and she pouted as her wound began to bleed. Then she yelled for her mother as she ran off.

"What's happened?" her mother yelled.

"It's Master Douggie. He pushed me down while we were playing and he's hurt me!"

"Master Burgess, get over here right now," her mother demanded. Such was my first encounter with a woman scorned, though at the time I knew nothing of such things. All I knew was that I was going to be in trouble over this. She told me that her husband would be back from the city shortly and he would address whatever problem Janet and I had.

I knew he would not go easy on me and I prepared for the worst. I decided not to defend myself or try to explain what had happened and how Janet had forced me to kiss her. Somehow, I knew I had crossed some important line in life's adventures that couldn't be addressed directly. It was only an issue between Janet and me, which could not be arbitrated by any adults. Janet looked at me with the same understanding that declared neither she nor I could speak the truth of what had happened.

Yet, for the first time in my life, I felt a rush of excitement that I could not explain. Janet's sparkling eyes and rosy pink cheeks, her sheer exuberance, thrilled me as never before. I had never really paid her that much attention and regarded her sister even less. We all had frolicked and played childish games, but it was not until that moment that I realized that this tomboy was really a girl! All I can say is that after that moment I could never deal with her in the same way again. Strange as it seemed to me, she liked and even encouraged this change of attitude. She was an older woman after all, being all of twelve while I was nine going on ten.

But why had this suddenly happened? Only a few days before I had never given her much thought at all. Sure, I had been excited about going on this trip. My parents were going to the Continent for a couple of weeks and Janet's father, Les, suggested that I come with his family on a "working man's holiday"—whatever that meant. Yet, here I was in the throes of a dilemma that I knew not the outcome. If this was indeed part of a "working man's holiday," I wanted nothing to do with it!

Les was a former Sergeant Major and "Desert Rat" in the British 8th Army under Montgomery. He was a veteran of the El Alemein campaign and had faced Rommel, the "Desert Fox" many a time. He worked with my father at the U.S. Embassy in London and they were war buddies as my father had also served in North Africa. Les had a great fondness for me and treated me like the son he wished he had. He had suffered a wound in North Africa, which left a large knob on the back of his neck. He used to enjoy playing a game with us where he would say, "Watch this!" He then would raise his head back so you could see his large Adam's apple. Then he would pretend to hit his Adam's apple very hard and jerk his head down and, behold, there was his Adam's apple on the back of his neck! The girls and I would laugh uproariously at this antic. It proved a winner every time.

There was no American school for dependents of U.S. Military personnel in London, so I had been enrolled in an English school called Marleybone not far from Regent's Park and the Crescent, where my family took up residence. Les and his family lived nearby and his two daughters also attended Marleybone. An arrangement had been made that I should go to their home after school and stay over for dinner with them until my parents could pick me up. Many a time, I recall while walking from school to within a block or so of Les and his wife Mary's flat of smelling the strong odor of mutton. (It's the only meat you can taste without eating it. The smell permeates your very inner being until you feel like bleating.)

Meanwhile, I could not help but fear what Les would think. Would he believe that I would intentionally push any girl out of anger, much less his own daughter? Soon, I could hear the putter of his Morris Minor roll up on the lot next to the beach. I saw Les waving excitedly as he ran towards us. "I've got presents," he said. "Gifts for you from town!"

Our moods changed with the excitement of the moment as we anticipated the gifts we might receive. From behind his back Les pulled out one doll and then another which he gave his daughters. Then in a more serious tone of voice he said, "As for you Master Douggie, I have a special gift." He reached slowly behind his back and pulled out a pearl handled pocketknife. "This is for you, your first pocket knife—the Excalibur of the working man!"

My heart sank as I was choked up and I said, "I cannot accept it!"

"And why not, lad? What's the matter?"

"It's because of what's happened between Janet and me!"

"And just what can that be?"

Mary interceded. "Master Burgess got rough with Janet and pushed her down on the rocks and hurt her."

Before I could say anything Janet blurted, "It's all my fault. I called him a sissy for not playing beach volley ball with me, so don't blame him. I egged him on. It is I who should give back the gift not him."

"Now children," Les said. "Let's not bicker. I don't think it's that important if no one got hurt. Let me see your scrape, Janet. Not so bad," he said. "And now Master Douggie. You know what they say about sticks and stones. Let's all apologize and get on with it, and let's start looking for wood on the beach so we can have a campfire tonight. All right, get a move on, will you!" With that, my heart lightened. I was exonerated.

Today I have a heavy-duty Swiss Army knife that has tweezers, scissors, five blades in varying lengths from two to four-and-a-half inches, a corkscrew and two different screwdrivers, as well as a toothpick. No matter how many features this knife possesses, it can never replace the memories of that day at the White Cliffs of Dover when I got my first pocketknife—and my first kiss from a girl.

Long Shots

❧

A couple of days ago a horse named Lethargic won the second race at Golden Gate Fields. It was a twenty-seven to one long shot. A two-dollar bet would have gotten you $54. It was the kind of horse my father would have bet on, but not my mother.

In 1950 the track wasn't too far from our Army housing in Richmond. Every couple of weeks we would go to the races and I would enjoy the hot dogs, pop and candy and get wound up in the excitement of the crowd at the track. Even then I could tell they were a bunch of characters.

My mother, all four feet, ten inches and ninety pounds of her, would head out from our seats to seek one of the local racing form barkers to see what the hot horse was for the day. One of her favorite taps was Hank who wore a straw hat with flyers sticking out of the brim.

"Get your hands out of your pocket and put your money to work on one of my picks!"

"Who's hot today, Hank?" she'd ask.

"Cruz'n Kitty in the fourth is a five to one shot. She placed second the other day on a wet track at one hundred and fifteen, today the track is clear and the jockey's at one hundred and ten pounds!"

"Sure thing, Hank?"

He gave her the thumbs up as he grabbed a racing forum and sold it to mom.

"I'm countin' on you, Hank!"

Mom followed the horses, jockeys, racing records, like a World Series buff who knew all the stats. After her rounds she would head back to the stands to see what my father and I were up to. We had been picking our own horses the way Dad saw it. He was not scientific. He'd watch the horses prancing out during the preview and see which ones were feisty or if he liked their markings or the colors of the jockeys' outfits. No racing form for him. No insight from the barkers touting their picks. It was all instinct— a combination of hunch and luck.

"Look at number nine, he looks part Appaloosa and part Pinto and his name is Tonto. Look at him prance, the jockey can't keep him under control, he'll be chomping at the bit before he gets out of the gate! He's also a fifteen to one shot, we'll make $30 bucks on every buck we bet!"

We thought we had a real winner, then mom said, "Who ya bettin' on?"

Dad said, "Tonto."

"What? That horse is too much of a long shot. Go with Cruz'n Kitty at five to one."

Mom would have nothing to do with Tonto. Dad didn't even recall what that horse looked like and mom wasn't there to see the preview. She was scientific, just the stats please! They went to the box office and placed their individual bets.

Dad said, "It's a sure thing. Tonto's ready to go." As we got back to our seats the horses were just entering the gate. Sure enough, Tonto was fussing and rearing. Cruz'n Kitty looked very svelte and sedate in her shiny black coat.

The shot rang out and they were off. Tonto exploded from the gate and took first place. Dad was shouting, "Go Tonto go." His face turned from pink to red. Mom was calm and collected as Cruz'n Kitty was now seventh from the pack of ten. As they rounded the first turn, Tonto was still in first and Mom's bet had pulled to fifth. By the second turn, Tonto was slipping to second while Cruz'n Kitty had gained to third. By the next corner, Tonto and Cruz'n Kitty were neck and neck.

There was a glimmer in Mom's eye as Dad's voice faded along with his horse. By the final turn, Mom's horse took the lead and kept pulling away. Tonto slipped to third, then fourth. Cruz'n Kitty won by two lengths. Tonto came in seventh.

Dad said nothing. Mom went to collect her winnings, while Dad was philosophical as he reminded us that Tonto would learn, and next time he would make his move later—no outta the gate first—when he heard the shot.

Mom had no excuses, she had won. When she came back from the box office she was flashing the winning bills much the same way Hank had held the forum flyers he pulled from his hat. Mom looked straight at me and said, "Remember son, you should always bet in the middle of the pack. Favorites won't make you rich and long shots are sucker bets. The next time we have a card party I want you to fill in and if Dad folds early, I want you to be my partner. He plays cards for social reasons, I play to win! I think you like to play like me! I'll show you how."

Somehow, that day, I found out who wore the pants in the family. My mom always held the winning hand. My dad continued to bet on the long shots. Neither worried about it—and that was the secret to their marriage.

Sue Hummel

Sue Hummel began writing stories at age eleven and just never stopped "scribbling." She earned her B.A. in English from Vassar College and later graduated with a M.L.S. from Columbia University, working as a librarian in the New York Public Library for nine years.

Since then, Sue has written and illustrated *The Cow Who Wanted to be an Elephant* and illustrated *The Twinkle Stars*, both self-published picture books, and she has added editing fiction and non-fiction to her literary repertoire.

Currently, Sue is working on a volume of short fiction. She lives with her husband and two cats in Concord, California.

Alice and Margaret

◆

1947

"Today I go to school," sang Alice. The little song danced in Alice's head as she dressed in her pleated green skirt, new blouse with narrow pink and green stripes and shiny green shoes. Mommy had told her about kindergarten, where she and other children her own age would play wonderful games together and learn their ABC's and 123's. Alice had only a moment to wonder why Margaret wasn't starting school too, then it was time to eat breakfast and go.

The night before, Alice and Margaret talked about school starting the next day. Alice usually could read Margaret's mind, but this time she couldn't. "Don't you want to start school, too?" she asked.

"Who needs Kindergarten?" Margaret said. She sounded upset. Alice wasn't sure why. She knew that Mommy and Daddy never noticed Margaret or talked to her.

Ever since she could remember, Alice knew Margaret was with her all the time, as certain as her own hands and feet. Margaret's thoughts and feelings were as clear to Alice as her own. It took her by surprise today when she didn't know why Margaret was upset about going to school.

There were other times when Margaret would hide herself. This made Alice nervous. She was relieved when she heard Margaret's voice again, making remarks about whatever was happening.

When Alice and her mother reached the school, they entered a large, bright classroom, with inviting small tables and chairs, and lots of comfy pillows on the floor. She saw a blackboard on one wall, and shelves of brightly-colored picture books, toys and even a live mouse in a cage. Alice was enthralled. In the center of the room, they met a tall, pretty lady with smooth, blonde hair. Mommy told Alice, "This is Mrs. Carter, your teacher." Alice gazed around at the other children. They smiled back.

Mommy left, promising to come back for her that afternoon. Alice listened while Mrs. Carter read a story to the class and they all sang *"Old MacDonald."* Alice knew all of the words. *I bet Margaret will like school,* she thought. She was so busy, she forgot about Margaret for the rest of the day.

1946

When Alice was four and her younger brother Ken was still a baby, their family moved to a big old house in town. Alice remembered their cottage near Grandma Helen, but she wasn't sorry to leave it. Now she had a bigger bedroom and a backyard that stretched far behind their house. They'd lived three other places that Alice remembered. Margaret shared the bedroom with her, the way she did wherever they lived. The girls loved to pretend a scary creature lived under their bed and came out at night. Alice called it 'a mountain-lion-bear.' It made growling noises while the two girls shrieked and pretended to be frightened.

All summer, she and Margaret played in the yard and watched her Daddy and Grandpa build a new family room in place of the dark, closed-in back porch. "This house is called a 'fixer-upper,' " Margaret said.

One day while the men were sawing and hammering in the yard, Margaret and Alice took an open bucket of white paint and two brushes to paint the outside wall of the new added-on room. They loved the clean smell of new wood in the room, and slapping paint on it—they could barely reach the siding—felt like an important job. A lot of white paint dripped on the ground. Alice knew that painting was Margaret's idea.

When Daddy found out that they were painting the house, he was very angry. Alice looked around, but Margaret had vanished and left Alice to face Daddy alone. He scolded her and sent her to her room.

Often, the two girls played a store game around the roots of the huge, shady tree at the far end of the back yard. Under its branches and lacework of green leaves, they were out of sight of the house. They took turns being the customer and the counter person of their store, using an old bench to set out their dirt cakes. It was strange, but lately when Alice saw Margaret, she looked transparent. Alice could see flowers and grass right through her.

1945

One morning after Alice's third birthday party, Mommy said, "Your Daddy's coming home soon." Alice was happy to hear this, because she knew her Daddy had been away in the war for a long time. Neither Alice nor Margaret really knew what a war was. They only knew that Daddy went away before they were born. Alice knew he was a very important person to Mommy, but she wasn't sure what a Daddy was. She asked Margaret, who said, "I think Daddy is the man who used to live with Mommy before we came."

Mommy acted happy and excited all the time. She put up new curtains in the windows and did some extra cleaning in their home. They had moved into a tiny house in the country, far away from all the grandparents. Alice wondered if a Daddy was better than a new book, a new toy, or a party. Margaret stood up tall and said, "We'll just have to wait and see." She could sound grown-up at times.

At last, Daddy arrived. He was bigger and taller than Alice or even Mommy. He had soft brown hair and dancing brown eyes, like Alice's own. He had a rather thin face and a loud voice. But his beautiful brown uniform was the best of all. It had a shirt with long sleeves, a pair of long pants, and a big brown hat with a shiny dark brown bill for lifting it on and off his head. He let Alice try on the hat. It fell over her eyes.

Another good thing about Daddy was that he gave Alice soda and potato chips, which she shared with Margaret. Mommy had never allowed her to drink soda or eat potato chips, saying it wasn't healthy, but Daddy said it was okay once in awhile. Alice treasured the first sweet sip of soda, straight from the glass bottle. And the crispety-crunch of each chip sang a little song to her.

Mommy and Daddy seemed to spend all their time together. They hugged and kissed a lot. They even slept in the same bed at night. Alice felt a twinge of jealousy. She would have loved to sleep with Mommy. But she liked her own little bed where she and Margaret often talked until Alice fell asleep. Sometimes she knew what Margaret was going to say before she said it, and of course, Margaret could tell what Alice was thinking.

The door to her parents' bedroom was open at night because the summer was sweltering hot; they hoped for a breeze. Alice overheard her Daddy say, "Sally, I am so sorry I wasn't here when the baby was born. It was very hard to leave you and go halfway around the world." Mommy said, "You know, Alice has been good company since she arrived."

In Alice's room, Margaret punched the pillow and muttered, "I was there too. I *am here*." Soon after Daddy came, they moved out of the house in the country and started driving back to Grandma and Grandpa's. On this trip, they stayed overnight at a city hotel. Late that evening, Mommy woke up Alice, put on her sweater over her pajamas, and brought her outdoors to the sidewalk into a wall of noise. Grown-ups danced, shouted, honked their car horns and set off firecrackers. Alice saw other little kids and older kids too. It was a huge outdoor party. Alice asked Margaret what was going on, but Margaret didn't have anything to say about this celebration. Instead, she was completely silent. Alice looked around, but Margaret had vanished.

Mommy and Daddy said to Alice, "Remember this night. The war is over, and our side won. This is a very important night." Alice tucked this information away with her important memories.

1944

Alice loved picture books more than anything, except maybe chocolate cake. Every Christmas or on her birthday, she could hardly wait to unwrap her presents, hoping for a new book. She'd learned to listen carefully to each story, and if her Mommy or another grown-up read it to her a few times, she could turn the pages and tell the story herself.

When she was two, her Daddy sent her a beautiful picture book about all the animals that lived in Australia, the country where he stayed during the war. The black swan, kangaroo, wallaby, koala bear, kookaburra, and duck-billed platypus romped through its pages. Margaret learned the names of the animals even quicker than Alice did. When they looked at the book together, Margaret turned the pages really fast.

1943

Alice sat at the edge of the white bedspread on her mother's big, soft bed, using both hands to hold a brush with a long handle and stiff bristles at one end. She waved it around and leaned forward. The world did a somersault, and she landed on the thin carpet covering the bedroom floor. The carpet bumped hard against her face—*Ow!* Alice was so surprised that she began to cry. Mommy rushed in, and said, "Oh, Alice. Are you all right?" Of course she wasn't all right. That hurt.

As her Mommy placed her back on the big bed, Alice caught an indignant look from Margaret, who was sitting quietly on the other side of the bed near the wall. Mommy hugged Alice and cooed, "It's going to be okay." But she placed Alice farther away from the edge.

After Mommy left the room again, Margaret made a face at her and said, "That was really dumb. You know better than to fall off the bed. Where is that brush now?" But Mommy had taken the brush and put it on a dresser top, where Alice couldn't reach it.

Margaret was about her own size and often sat on the big bed with her, though Mommy didn't seem to notice her or talk to her. Margaret usually wore the same kinds of clothes Alice wore. Her brown hair was caught up in a little bow, just like Alice's hair.

The next morning, Mommy put Alice's first real dress on her. It was gorgeous yellow, but prickly and stiff. Margaret wore a dress just like it, but it wasn't hurting her, apparently. Margaret laughed when Alice squirmed to get more comfy.

"You look very pretty," Mommy said. "If only you didn't have that black eye from falling on the floor. I guess you can come to Henny's wedding anyway."

That same morning, all the grownups in the house went next door to the huge, dark building where every week her Grandfather stood behind a tall desk and talked to the many people. Today, while Alice, Mommy and Grandma sat with other grown-ups on wooden benches, her Aunt Henny and a strange man stood in front of her Grandfather, and they all said a lot of words. Then her Grandfather said something and the couple exchanged rings and kissed each other, pecking on the lips. After that, they turned and walked down the aisle and out of the building while the rest of the people followed and threw rice at them. Alice knew it was rice because she had eaten some in her pudding for dessert.

Summer, 1942

Light . . . dark . . . light . . . whenever she was awake, she sensed the same huge face, warm voice, soft arm and cheek in the dim room with the big, soft bed.

Alice was aware of several Big Ones besides the Main One, this most important grown-up who was with her nearly all the time, day and night. At night, the Main One put her into a soft little bed in a corner of the same room. Alice's coverlet was cozy. She was sleepy, full of milk, and very happy. Only sometimes, near her on the same bed, she noticed another baby girl who never made a sound.

1942

"Oh—the baby is coming." Sally was startled awake from a nap and realized her water had broken. The sheets were soaked. But by her calculations, the baby was at least a week early.

It was noon on a sunny, cold Monday in April and she was alone in her parents' home beside Trinity Episcopal Church. Her father, a minister, was at a special luncheon in his honor; her mother was shopping downtown with friends. Her sister was teaching high school in a nearby city.

After she cleaned up in the bathroom, Sally dressed and grabbed the little suitcase she kept packed and ready. She phoned for a cab. This was not the way she had pictured her baby's arrival!

She had the presence of mind to call Dr. Marcus and say she was going to the hospital; then her contractions began in earnest. Propping herself against a chair, Sally gasped until each one subsided. Whenever she could breathe normally and talk, she got the operator to call the telephone numbers for her family. She phoned Steinbach's Department Store where her mother was shopping and had her paged. Right before the taxi pulled up outside the house, she left a note on the hallway table:

"Gone to the hospital. Baby arriving. Come soon. S."

Riding on the gurney to the delivery room, Sally felt relief when Dr. Marcus rushed into the hall. He gave her hand a reassuring squeeze. "I'll check your vitals as soon as I slip into something less comfortable," he said.

Getting prepped, Sally was alternately wracked by labor contractions and sleepy from the shot given her to take the edge off her pain. Dr. Marcus walked in and assured her that everything "looked really good." Her last clear thought was, *Well, it better be good. This baby is coming now.*

When her surroundings swam back to her after the birth, Sally was exhausted, but felt tremendous relief. The worst part was over, and she was now a mom. Her only regret was that her husband, Frank, was many thousands of miles away, fighting the war in the Pacific.

She asked a nearby nurse, "Can I see my baby now? Is it healthy?" And almost an afterthought, "Do I have a girl or a boy?"

"She's beautiful, a healthy baby girl," replied the nurse with a big smile. Then with a serious look, she added, "Let me send the doctor in to see you."

Dr. Marcus entered and grasped her hand. He wasn't smiling. "There was something unexpected, Sally. Yes, you have a healthy girl, seven pounds, eight ounces. But she had a twin, another girl, who probably died before the birth. We didn't even know about her until the delivery."

Sally was speechless. Her first thought was: *Twins?* No one in her family or Frank's family had ever had twins that she knew.

"Your sister just got here. You can see her now," Dr. Marcus said.

Henny rushed in, and hugged Sally hard. "Oh—a niece! How wonderful!"

"Yes . . . but there were two, Henny. Twins. One died." Sally couldn't continue.

For a moment, Henny was lost for words. Then she said, "Did you and Frank pick out names?"

"Yes. Kenneth or Frank for a boy. For a girl, Alice or Margaret."

After the Fight

❦

I woke up and didn't know where I was. My head and left shoulder burned like fire. My left leg felt broken. I lay on a wooden floor and recognized the smells of the shed at the boatyard, where I hang out a lot. The thick, rancid smell of oil and the biting odor of cleaning fluid enveloped me.

I tried to open my eyes, but only the right one worked and I could see a little. The left eye felt glued shut. I saw boating equipment and nautical spare parts. I was near the back of the shed. Some fresh air blew through a crack beneath the door. Was it a windy day? Hard to tell.

As I moved my head and neck, pain shot through me, cautioning me to take it slow. My left shoulder throbbed and burned. I tried to peek at it from my right eye, but could not turn my head.

Now I remembered the brawl with my sworn enemy. I don't know his name, but I call him The Ugly Bastard, though I don't know anything about his lineage or parentage. We were having one of our regular fights. He punched at my head and hit my left eye. Lights out!

What a lousy business. I admit that life on the streets is rough, but this was an especially bad break for me. If I'm really crippled, how will I get enough to eat and drink? How will I survive?

From the corner of my eye, I saw there was no one else in the shed. It was quiet in there, but I heard voices outside in the boat yard.

When I moved my body, horrible pain in my shoulder and leg stopped me. Something was broken, I was sure of it. After a few minutes, I moved again. This time, I raised my body enough to drag it across the floor toward the door. I struggled a few feet, and then rested. Finally, I reached the door and opened it a crack. Summoning all my strength, I pushed the door open far enough to drag myself outside and onto the dirt and gravel of the boat yard.

The sun was blinding; it was perhaps mid-afternoon on a very warm late spring day. Sunshine dazzled and danced on the water of the harbor and bounced off the bright, painted motorboats and sailboats berthed side-by-side along every pier. In the background, I heard the continuous growls of boat motors as crafts left the harbor or returned to their berths. I had to stop again, panting, until the pain subsided.

Across the yard, two guys stood on the deck of their boat, a small sailboat in dry dock. They had climbed a ladder up its side. Their radio played rock music, and they called to one another as they worked.

If I could get their attention, maybe one of them would bring me the medical help I desperately needed. Gathering all my energy, I pushed my body up on my arms.

"Meow!" I hollered.

Playing the President

❖

The September sun had already set when the Ziegfeld Follies opened that evening in Baltimore. Across the alley from the theater's stage door, a pale western sky outlined chimneys and rooftops. Bill stood inside the door and watched the silhouette of a lone gull flying above peaked roofs. Up and up it circled, out of sight.

Bill's thoughts drifted to Long Island, to Betty and the kids. How Betty had smiled when he told her the Follies were booked in Baltimore to play for President Wilson. "You'll be great. I'm sure of it!" For a moment he could feel her hand squeeze his.

He wiped sweat from his forehead. Why was he always so nervous before every performance? He moved back into the narrow hall to the shared dressing room. Somewhere ahead a door opened to backstage, and he caught the strains of Willie Collier's music. "Always lead with the best," George M. Cohan said. Just like baseball, you lead with a batter who will get on base. The door closed and the orchestra grew faint. He listened for Collier's first laughs. With President Wilson out front, he wanted to know how the audience responded to Collier. After George M. Cohan, Collier's was the biggest name in the show.

Bill considered going backstage to watch the acts. He wasn't due onstage for almost two hours. But he'd get even more nervous hanging around in the wings. He lounged against the wall, pulled at his right earlobe a few times, and waited for someone, anyone to come along the hall so he could strike up a conversation. At last, Bill walked to the dressing room he shared with a few other cast members. Strewn with costumes, street clothes and overflowing ashtrays, the dressing room reeked of greasepaint, hair tonic, smoke, and sweat. Now the room was deserted except for an ancient juggler who'd turned comedian in order to keep eating.

"Frank, when do you go on?"

"Ten minutes. Oh, it's you." Frank stared at his reflection in the mirror dabbing a red dot of greasepaint beside each eye.

"Have you heard anything about how the audience is receiving us?" Bill said.

"What's the matter? Getting nervous?" Frank said. He seemed too nervous to talk with the stars, Collier and GM, but he acted comfortable with Bill.

"Well God Almighty, that's the big boss out there. I can't stop thinking that tonight I take my life in my hands."

"You think you've got good stuff? Good jokes?"

"I sure hope so," Bill said.

"Then go out there and give 'em some laughs." Frank turned to look at Bill.

"Maybe I'll practice. Right now I'm about to collapse."

"Didn't you say there's no way to practice?" asked Frank.

"Oh, I don't mean the jokes. They have to be spontaneous. I mean my rope tricks. I may need 'em tonight if the audience is tough."

Bill shook his head. He walked to the closet door and removed his lariats from the doorknob. He held the rope coils in his left hand and shook out the lasso with his right. He examined the knot to make sure it was firm. He spun the loop and it opened, first down near the floor in front of him, then parallel to his head. He moved it overhead, still spinning.

"It's a wonder how you make that rope behave," Frank said with near-reverence.

"Something to do," Bill said and flushed with pride. All of a sudden the rope hit the ceiling of the room, glanced off, then slapped on the floor. "If that ain't bad luck, I don't know what is." Bill coiled the lariat, replaced it on the closet doorknob, and checked his watch.

"Why don't you sit down and relax?" Frank had finished powdering over his makeup, looking at it one last time.

"If there was a train leaving for Long Island in fifteen minutes, I'd be on it." Bill sat down.

"We're all running the risk that the President won't like our stuff," Frank said.

"But you're not about to die for kidding your country and your president. "

"With all that's happening in the world, I'm sure you have good material."

"The war in Europe, the U.S. Army skirmishing with Mexicans at the border, and note-passing between Austria and Germany-—I've got plenty. I just don't know if he'll laugh at himself."

"You're on in three, Mr. Porter," Sam Goodrich called through the door.

"That's it. Gotta go." Frank eased out of his seat and walked to the door, his stride stiff and his shoulders drawn up close to his neck. He looked old and helpless. "See you after the show, Rogers."

"Right." Bill imagined himself a Christian in a Roman arena where, all too soon, lions would be loosed on him. He had only his wits and lariat for protection.

Once Frank's footsteps faded, Bill paced the room and rubbed the back of his neck with vigor. Soon he would need another haircut. For something to do, he removed his suit and shirt and began to don his cowboy outfit.

Recalling that he was billed as the Cherokee Kid in his early rodeo days, he felt a twinge of embarrassment when putting on the showy cowboy shirt, tight pants, chaps and high-heeled boots which went with the lariat tricks. *This isn't truly me now*, he thought. *I can do the tricks if I don't wear a thing. "Come one, come all! See the Naked Cherokee Kid."* He grinned as he put on his costume. That would sure rile up the Ziegfeld Follies chorus girls, who made their living dancing in scanty costumes.

126

"Oh, what the hell, it'll be over in a few hours," Bill said aloud.

Tonight it took him a little longer to dress. He noticed a dark stain on his left shirtsleeve. He went to the sink, grabbed a towel and tried to wash it out, but the stain didn't dissolve.

Bill stood before Frank's mirror. As always, tousled brown hair, weather-creased face and silver-blue eyes met him. He saw the same mouth with lines of age and laughter at its corners. His hair and makeup were simple, but he hated greasepaint. He dabbed a bit on his face before he stopped in disgust. *If they don't like my face, that's their problem, not mine.*

He wandered around the room again. *How is the show going? I wish to God someone would come back here and talk.* He paused beside the chair where he had deposited his street suit. He picked up the jacket and folded it with more care. Betty would approve. She always got after him for making a mess of his clothes. There had been a time when he cared a lot about keeping his clothes neat and attractive. When he was cakewalk champion in Oklahoma and Texas, fresh from winning the biggest roping and calf-tying event in the largest rodeo in Oklahoma, he had cared a lot more. Was he already thirty-six now? It didn't seem possible.

Bill looked again at his reflection. His outfit was complete except for the wide-brimmed, white Stetson he donned right before going onstage.

With a jolt, Bill remembered President Wilson out front. Tightness returned to his chest. He took a few deep breaths, as GM had taught him to do when he got the heebie-jeebies before a performance. He heard tapping on the dressing room door.

"You in there, Rogers?"

"Yes sir."

The door opened and George M. Cohan appeared, small, slender and dapper. His light, graying hair was slicked close to his head. His pale eyes twinkled as he looked at Bill.

"How is the show goin'?" Bill said.

"All right, I guess. No complaints, kid. But you sound edgy."

"Every time I think of President Wilson out front, I get weak in the knees. He might just retaliate for all the jokes I've told on him, by not laughing." Bill looked down at the scuffed toes of his boots.

"Aw, come on kid, he loves it," GM said. "He's eating it up."

"Well, that's all your stuff. Who wouldn't go for that?"

"Rogers, you're a worrier. Mr. Wilson happens to have a great sense of humor. He laughs even at the lines he's not supposed to laugh at." Cohan put a hand on Bill's shoulder. His smile was broad and reassuring, as self-satisfied as he was sympathetic. "Everything's rosy, just rosy. Calm down."

GM Cohan had no worries. He was a mainstay of the Follies. He had been born into vaudeville. "If I could dance as good as my old man," he'd said, "I wouldn't have to spend my time writing corny lyrics and tunes."

If! More than once, Bill had felt a twinge of envy when he saw GM's graceful glides and flashy dance moves. His own cakewalking days were long past, but he still bounced his foot when he heard a catchy tune.

GM looked at Bill with a quizzical smile. "Come on, Rogers, he won't bite. I'll have to introduce you to him after the show."

Bill nodded.

"Anyhow, I gotta go. I'm on in a couple of minutes. See you later." He strode to the door and left, raising a hand in farewell.

"Thanks for stopping by," Bill called after him.

Under the harsh bulb, he looked at his watch. 9:45 p.m. He was due onstage in half an hour, right after the intermission at ten. His mouth and throat felt dry. He walked to the little sink, turned on the cold-water faucet, cupped his hands under the stream, then drank. The water was warm and tasted bad.

What else to do? He refused to go through the sections of today's newspaper that lay scattered among clothes on the floor. Instead, he felt in his pockets for his chewing gum. During his act, he could get a laugh by taking the chewed gum out of his mouth and sticking it on the side of the stage, the proscenium arch, and then taking it back and popping it into his mouth when he walked offstage at the end.

"Not sanitary," Betty commented. But it sure didn't hurt anything, and a few people even said they came in order to see him do that. Now there were just two sticks of gum in the little wrapper in his shirt pocket. Bill folded one stick into his mouth, and wadded up its individual wrapper. He stuck this into one of the overflowing ashtrays. He could hear laughing and clapping out front for GM's songs and jokes. Bill chewed, snapped and smacked his gum. It did help to calm him.

Bill noticed that he or Cohan had left the dressing room door ajar. He stuck his head out to see if anyone was nearby to talk to.

"Sir, have you seen my father?" asked a small voice which seemed to come from beside Bill. He took a few steps back into the dressing room, and looked down. A boy with dark, wide eyes stood looking at him. He spoke again, his pronunciation crisp and clipped for Baltimore.

"I said, have you seen my father, sir?"

Bill opened the door wider. In the yellowish light he saw a boy with neat knickers buckled at the knee and spotless shoes. He wore a shirt and suit jacket with a small bow tie.

"Who's your father?"

"Dr. Graham. Dr. Martin Graham. If you've been in Baltimore any length of time, you've heard of him."

"I'm sorry I don't know him. I'm travelling with this show."

"He said he was going to the performance at 8:30. I went to the theater's front doors and they wouldn't let me in to look for him." There was a slight hitch in his voice.

"You better come in and sit down for a minute," Bill said. "If your pa is watching this show, he may come out for air at the intermission. That's pretty soon now."

"I want to find him now," the boy said. He didn't budge. He scraped his left shoe back and forth on the floor. Bill saw he was close to tears.

"Like I told you, he's probably watching the show. You wouldn't want to spoil his fun, would you?"

No reply.

"He'll come out like I said, then you can watch the rest of the show with him. Reckon that'll do?" Bill forced a grin.

The boy pressed his lips together, then nodded.

"Now you can relax. Have you ever been in a real theater dressing room before?"

"Yes. Many times."

"You have?"

"Yes. My mom is an opera singer, who used to be called 'The Song Bird.' She doesn't sing much now, but I have been to her dressing room plenty of times."

"Okay. I meant one of these, where lots of performers change their costumes. That's what this room's for." He swept one arm wide to emphasize the dressing tables and costumes.

"Really?" the child replied, wiping his nose on his sleeve. He pushed his dark hair off his damp forehead.

"Yep. Want to come in and take a look?" Bill stepped to one side, and the boy entered. Bill controlled his desire to ask why this child was traveling alone at night. He wanted to say, "I bet you'd like my boy, Billy. He can ride a horse already, though he's a little younger'n' you."

"May I have a piece of your gum?" the boy asked.

"Was you watching me when I took out the gum?"

"Were," the child said. "*Were* you watching."

"Aw, come on in. I'll give you the gum."

They walked side by side through the room and sat in two chairs next to each other.

Bill waited while his small companion climbed onto the chair, then sat himself. He produced the flat gum package, extracted the last stick and offered it to the child.

With slow dignity, the boy accepted the gum and unwrapped it.

"Thank you." He put the gum into his mouth and handed the empty wrapper back to Bill, who pocketed it.

For a few moments they chewed in silence. The child looked around the disheveled room, wrinkled his well-shaped nose, and frowned.

"It smells in here, and it's not tidy."

"No time to clean up until the show is over," Bill said, putting his elbow on the nearest dressing table and leaning his cheek against his hand.

"My mother says there's always time to be tidy, unless you're lazy." He wagged his head up and down. He swung his legs. No danger of them reaching the floor.

Bill had the impression that he was not talking to an eight-year-old child, but to a midget, or other small adult. He heard a small snuffling and chewed his gum, pretending he hadn't noticed.

"Say, do you know the President of the United States is watching our show tonight, along with your father?" Bill said.

"I know. He isn't with my father, though. He doesn't know my father. I also came here tonight to see the President. He knows me."

"How come he knows you?"

"He shook hands with me once when I visited Washington last year. I want to see him again."

"How did you get here tonight?" Bill asked.

"I looked up the address of the theater in the newspaper, and I came in a taxicab. I used some money that my mother keeps in a book in our study. But I didn't have enough to pay for a ticket into the theater."

Bill nodded. "You know, I've never met Mr. Wilson. I'm kind of nervous about the show tonight, since I'm going to make some jokes about how he's running the country."

"He's a very nice man," the boy said. "I think he'll laugh. You should meet him sometime. Maybe I can introduce you to him."

Bill rubbed his hand across his mouth to hide a smile. "Maybe you can." He looked around the room for something else to talk about. His stomach felt tight. He saw it was nearly 10:00, time for the intermission.

"Why are you wearing those clothes?" the boy said. "I never saw anyone wear such silly clothes."

"I wear this outfit because I do rope tricks onstage. These are the clothes of a working cowboy. Where I come from, this is what you wear to do cowboy work. You would ruin an ordinary suit in a few hours living and working on a cattle ranch."

"Where are you from?"

"Out west. Indian Territory, now the state of Oklahoma."

"Are you a real cowboy? What do you do on a ranch?"

Bill relaxed and slouched a little on his chair.

"Rope and brand cattle, ride herd over them, and drive them to market." He didn't add that since he was working full time in the Follies, he didn't go back to cattle ranching.

The boy seemed to look at Bill's outfit with new interest.

"These are chaps," said Bill. "They protect your legs against the horns of the steers and plants like cactus."

"I bet they're hot to wear," the boy said.

"Yep. I take them off when I'm done with my act."

"So you wear this whole costume just to do rope tricks?"

"The point is, I do something nobody else does in the show. I tell jokes and swing my lariat."

The child looked around the room. Spying the lariat, he slid off his chair and trotted over to the rope. He examined it with careful fingers and found the loop. He pulled at its knot. "Is this your rope?"

"Yup."

"Show me how it works."

He brought the lariat to Bill, who stood up and stretched. He took the rope from the boy and shook out the loop, then beckoned the boy to take a seat. Bill·spun the loop near the floor at first. He savored the hiss of the whirling rope and pull of centrifugal force on his arm. As he lifted his end of the rope, the loop rose above his head. He lowered it again to his knees, and he jumped in and out of the loop, his feet together, in and out, in and out. Then he twirled it away. With a swift motion of his wrist, he dropped it over the seated boy's head. The loop first rose again into the air, then slapped down and caught the child's shoulders, fastening him to his chair. The boy went wide-eyed.

Bill walked along his rope, coiling it up as he went, and then slipped the loop back over the child's head.

"Did you learn that when you were a cowboy?" The boy's eyes stayed on the lariat.

"I practiced a lot," Bill said. "But that's all it takes. Practice." He ran his hand over the smooth rope. Even while he recalled President Wilson in the audience, his lariat bolstered his confidence.

"Could I learn to do that?"

Bill grinned. "Well, I guess so. You're older'n' I was when I starting swingin' a rope."

"I'll be nine in November. I asked for a pony for my birthday, so I'll ride, too."

"Good. And a rope isn't hard to come by. A clothesline will do for a start. Watch out for the furniture if you practice in the house. Roping people ain't appreciated, even though it's great practice. They generally don't like it."

They were quiet. Bill grinned and reached over to the boy and mussed his hair.

The boy smiled. *He must feel safe here*, Bill thought.

"Rogers!" There was a knock on the door. "Intermission's almost over. You got six minutes!"

"Who was that?" the boy said.

"That's Sam Goodrich. He tells us when it's time to go onstage. Thanks, Sam!"

"Intermission! My daddy came out of the theater!" The boy slid off his chair. "Can we find him now?"

"Sure. We can go around front." The boy was already trotting to the door. He was short for almost nine, but solidly built. Bill decided he would be good on a pony.

The boy ran ahead of Bill out the stage door into the starlit alley, and around to the crowded theater entrance. Most of the audience had come out for fresh air and was heading back to their seats. The rustling of ladies' silks and the penguin black-and-white tuxedos of the gentlemen made Bill chuckle inwardly. They all glittered under the lights: painted, gay, important. He knew they read the Washington and Baltimore papers each day and pretended to care about the war in Europe. For a moment

Bill scanned for President Wilson and his secret service men. Then he realized they probably wouldn't come out of the theater.

The boy stood with his head flung back, chin thrust out, searching for his dad. With a sudden cry of "Daddy!" he plunged into the retreating crowd without another glance at Bill. *I don't even know his name*, Bill thought.

He turned and walked back into the alley and then to the stage door. By his watch, he had about half a minute before he went backstage. Away from the brightly lit marquis, the shuffle and babble of the elite of Baltimore and Washington, he remembered the President. Ducking into the dressing room, he grabbed his white Stetson and ropes. He strode out into the dingy hall, grinning, eyes dancing, to perform for President Wilson and a nameless boy.

Holding Hands

❦

August, 1990

"Good afternoon, AIDS Hospice of San Francisco," says a crisp female voice.

"Hello. Do you have Andrew Carlson there as a patient?"

"Let me check. Yes, we do. What is your business?"

"I'm his sister. I'd like to speak with him now if I may."

"Hold on, please. I'll put you through."

In the silence while my call connects, I try to visualize my younger brother. Tall, slender, auburn-haired and freckled, I haven't laid eyes on him for at least fifteen years.

"Hello? Nance?" I don't recognize the voice at first. It's softer and weaker than I remember.

"Drew, yes. It's me. I'm here in town. May I visit you today or tomorrow?"

A pause, the strange voice replies, "Well, sure. This afternoon works for me." His coughing fit is painful to hear.

"Drew? Are you sure it's okay?"

"Yeah. I'm not going anywhere."

"Okay. How about three o'clock?"

"Great. I'm looking forward to it."

"Okay, so long until then."

"Bye." He sounds out of breath. We hang up.

I don't know San Francisco at all. My family and I live in Chicago. That's where Drew and I grew up. I take a taxi and arrive at the hospice on time. Since our phone call, I have been trying to attach the whispery voice on the phone with Drew, the darling boy, then the teenager who topped six feet.

When I was fourteen and he turned twelve, we were almost the same height, but he continued sprouting. A few times we attended the same high school dances, and being very popular, he would introduce me as his younger sister.

One evening during my senior year, Drew took me into his bedroom and shut the door. He acted nervous. I didn't know what to expect. "Nance, I have to tell you something, but you can't tell anyone, not Mom and Dad or anyone." His eyes were huge.

"Well, what is it?" I didn't sound very sensitive right then.

"I'm in love with David, a kid in my class." He looked miserable. I sat suddenly on the nearest chair. The safe world of our childhood came crashing down. Drew was the closest person to me in my life, and I'd never suspected. We talked for hours that night and I realized what a privilege and honor it was to be included in his most private world. He wanted my support. I did my best to reassure him that he was still a unique and precious person, and always would be.

After I graduated from high school, we grew apart. I attended four years of college, earning a B.A. in Journalism. He finished high school with honors, and continued on to university, majoring in electrical engineering. I heard from him occasionally, and he told me about his latest partner. He didn't settle down for a long time, but finally went to San Francisco, found and moved in with Bill.

I enter the hospice lobby, introduce myself to the desk attendant and ask where to find Andrew Carlson. The attendant gives me his room number, and points to the elevator. Even in the lobby, I am aware of a scrubbed, antiseptic odor. It reminds me of a hospital.

At his door, I knock twice. Someone opens right away, a middle-aged man in a health worker's uniform. His face is lined, tired-looking. "Nancy? Come in," he says, not waiting for an answer. I think my family resemblance to Drew is still obvious. When we were about the same height, we were taken for twins.

The room is spacious, with daylight pouring through one big window. It's got all the sickroom equipment, monitors, an IV, measuring instruments and medicines. I take it in with one glance.

Drew is sitting on the side of the hospital bed, dressed, his hair buzz-cut. He is awfully thin. "Nance? Oh it's good to see you!"

I choke back my dismay at how ill he looks. I rush over to hug him. He rises into my arms. Then we're both crying. He feels frail in my embrace.

"Why didn't you tell me?"

"I couldn't call," he mumbles into my hair. He utters no more words about his illness.

I find myself saying over and over, "It's all right, it's all right," and easing him back so he is sitting on the bed. Scenes flood into my memory from our past together. Years growing up, playing, going to the ocean, holding hands tightly as we jumped the waves or ducked under. A sharp feeling of "never again" almost overwhelms me. Funny, even though you realize you can't go back, at times like this it hits you over the head. Part of me knows that Drew will never leave this room.

"Nance, this is Howard," he introduces me to his health worker. I don't know what their exact relationship is. Right now, I don't care.

"I think I have to lie down," Drew says. I help him lie on the pillows Howard has fluffed up behind his head. Now I see the full extent of this wasting disease. His eyes are huge in his face. His skin is broken in ugly sores. His breath rasps in and out. His pants and shirt are too big for his shrunken body. For a long moment, we gaze at each other. Then I find a chair nearby and pull it over beside the bed, near his head.

"Well," I say, "This is the pits." I grab his nearest hand, the long, slim fingers swallowed in mine.

"Remember when we went to the beach and jumped the waves? Holding hands?"

Drew nods his head slightly. It's an effort.

"What was the song we sang?" I want him to say it.

"Come—and Dance with Me?"

"That's it." Holding hands very tightly, I begin the old, familiar song:

"Brother come and dance with me—both my hands I offer thee." And for a short, magical time, we are again two innocent, happy children, holding hands as we jump the waves.

Franklin T. Burroughs

Franklin T. Burroughs serves as Adjunct Professor at John F. Kennedy University in Northern California and as an English Language Officer (Contractor) with the U.S. Department of State. He holds a B.A. degree from Pepperdine College, an M.S. degree in Education from U.S.C. and an Ed.D. degree from U.C.L.A. He did post-doctoral work at the University of Tehran, Iran.

Franklin has published in many scholarly journals. His writings have also appeared in "Contra Costa Times" and "The Wall Street Journal." He is co-author of a short volume entitled *World of Learning: A Collection of Essays* and recently published his memoir under the title *The Pepper Tree Kingdom*. He is currently working on two books: *In the Land of Rumi* and *On Writing My Memoir.*

The Devil Dancers
on Route 66

◦◦

Clifford's father had a mission: to convert the world to the Jesus-only movement, which rejects the traditional Christian doctrine of the Triune God and promotes Jesus as the fullness of the godhead. His epiphany represented a mid-life experience; he tolerated few ideas that varied from his understanding of the gospel.

His father's vision focused on the narrow corridor known as Route 66. The family traveled that route from California to Arkansas and back several times each year, usually hurriedly, with a set itinerary. If the father did not have a preaching gig, they would stop only briefly to eat or rest.

His parents had originally followed Highway 66 from Arkansas to California during the Depression years. They were among the more than two hundred thousand individuals who escaped the anguish of the Dust Bowl in the 1930s by using that highway to pursue new opportunities in the West. The father often reiterated his escape from the financial and social prison of Arkansas during the thirties and his increasing anticipation of financial freedom as he approached California.

"There was nothing for us in Arkansas. The bank was foreclosing on our farm, and we were becoming poorer and poorer," his father would blabber. "Jobs were not available. I couldn't even find something to do as a laborer. The drought in Texas and Oklahoma made things even worse. California was our only hope, Route 66 the way of escape."

Clifford, a twelve-year-old tired of hearing the tale over and over again, never acknowledged his boredom to his father. He tolerated the much repeated account because he had learned in school that his mother and father had gone through very rough times in the early 1930s, and Route 66 had helped in the mobilization of manpower to the advantage of the many Dust-Bowl migrants.

Neither the flocks of colorful birds, nor the herds of nervous deer nor the appearance of name-brand products on roadside billboards distracted the father. Weariness would sometimes interrupt his concentration, prompting him to seek out the nearest motor hotel or motel, and announce to Clifford and Clifford's mother, "I'm tired. Let's sleep for three or four hours and then continue the trip." Clifford couldn't object; his age discouraged him from openly challenging his father's wishes. His mother never disputed what the father said. After all, the father was the driver and knew when he needed to rest.

The types of motels in which the parents collapsed briefly were designed for motorists and often consisted of a single building of connected rooms with doors facing a parking lot and a parking area for motor vehicles. The motels were quite inexpensive and readily accessible from the highway.

Clifford could seldom sleep during these relatively brief stopovers. His mother and father occupied the bed, and he was dumped on a cot brought in at the last minute by the on-duty manager of the motel. During the three or four hours his parents were resting, Clifford lay imagining he was occupying a luxurious suite in a five-star hotel on a South Pacific island or in a European capital city. His choice of islands or cities would be nothing short of erratic, but the choice helped him tolerate the uncomfortable cot until his parents were ready to get up and move on.

The father's timing and precise destination were irregular, but his mission was clear to him. He was selling the intangible merchandise of hope and eternal life. As the family traversed the deserts and penetrated the cities along the way, the father frequently reminded both the mother and Clifford that a particular trip was divinely ordained and inherently significant to their future, after-death reward.

At each stop along the evangelistic trail, the father would declare, "God has revealed a breakthrough in this town. He has promised to bless my preaching and greatly increase the number of believers. He has designated me to be his special messenger." The revelation and/or promise most often seemed to come through a conversation with a fellow evangelist or a dream.

Clifford remembered hearing this same pronouncement from early childhood, and by the time he reached twelve, he had begun to doubt its authenticity. Each time his father would reaffirm his special relationship with God, Clifford would roll his eyes and say to himself, "Why haven't you been more successful in attracting followers if God has ordained you to save souls and heal the sick? I never see more than forty people in your audience; few of them come forward for prayer." But he wouldn't say anything to his father. He kept his thoughts to himself.

Clifford often took his beloved cat, Fifi, on the evangelistic trips, and Fifi slept comfortably behind the back seat of the car. When she needed to urinate or defecate, she would meow and jump onto the back seat. The father resisted stopping for Fifi's need to relieve herself until her meows reached a pitch that he couldn't endure. At that point he would pull to the side of the road, command that Clifford and Fifi exit the car and exhort them to hurry. He would remind Clifford that an audience in Arkansas or along the way was eagerly awaiting the pitch for his intangible merchandise.

One stop for Fifi involved a particularly extended period of defecation, and the father became upset. He began to complain while Fifi insisted on thoroughly covering her feces. She couldn't seem to find enough dirt to complete her task and just kept scratching with her right paw. Finally, Clifford's father declared, "I can't wait any longer and am starting the car."

"Come on, Dad," Clifford pleaded. "You know cats are very particular about their surroundings and need their privacy when they have to go."

In an effort to intervene, Clifford announced that he also had to urinate and begged for a minute or two more. He could have waited for at least another hour before urinating, but he wanted to give Fifi enough time to finish her task. He whispered to Fifi, "You must rush just a bit. Dad is getting mad."

Clifford relieved himself as slowly as possible. He watched each drop of urine sink into the dirt, uniting the earth and his body with a signature of nature. He imagined that he was watering beautiful roses in a backyard garden with the colorless stream of water by creating a circle in the dust.

The father succumbed to the ploy; Clifford experienced perfect contentment in manipulating the father through natural processes. By the time he had finished relieving himself, Fifi had completed her task, and they both jumped into the car without any fanfare. As Clifford watched, Fifi settled into her usual spot and attempted to get comfortable. He pondered the enormity of the world, the beauty of the sun that beamed through the car windshield and surveyed the surrounding landscape. Unfortunately, the surroundings displayed little beauty. Everything was dry and brown. He hoped Fifi wouldn't need to relieve herself again for a while and wished for a more intriguing setting for his next natural signature. He whispered, "Fifi, I hope you don't have to go again until we stop for the night or Dad gets tired and wants to rest. I don't want Dad to tell me I have to give you to somebody else. That would break my heart. You know how much you mean to me." Fifi uttered a quiet "meow" and went to sleep. She began to purr as soon as her eyes were closed.

Clifford was seeking happiness but not really finding it while cooped up in his father's car. And he didn't think he had ever really experienced contentment during his childhood. He often dreamed of belonging to something or some group, but the family's continuous jaunts imprisoned him in his own dysfunctional world. His father's messianic excitement and animation frightened him. He felt the eye of God was constantly on him, daring him to do something contrary to God's will and worthy only of eternal punishment.

His father's rules were not always clear and certainly were discriminately applied. He could readily be punished for some behavior of which his father didn't approve but in which the father himself might have participated. At least the threat of punishment for an act the father considered anathema to his religious dogma constantly plagued Clifford. Even kissing a girl was considered a sin and worthy of fatherly as well as eternal punishment.

Clifford's mother could have been a member of the walking dead, behaving at times like Boris Karloff and not wanting in any way to challenge his father. At times, Clifford would stare at her, secretly asking her to say something or give an opinion. But she never responded to his indirect, non-verbal entreaties. She sat or stood like a deaf mute with her hands by her side, displaying an artificial Mona-Lisa smile without the mysterious demeanor. She wasn't afraid of the father but never felt it necessary to show any initiative or effort to curb the father's pharisaical approach to life and his legalistic relationship with Clifford.

Fifi the cat was the only being who provided Clifford any psychological solace between the relief and rest stops. Even though she was not a purebred, she had the characteristics of a Persian feline: a long flowing coat, a chunky body, stocky legs and big eyes set in a round, flat face. She was quiet, gentle, and undemanding. With Clifford particularly, she was playful and very affectionate. She gave Clifford much love and devotion, making up for some of his parents' lack of attention.

Unlike Clifford's father, Fifi readily adapted to almost any environment and seldom seemed upset. She loved to be stroked and petted and responded to the least bit of attention Clifford gave her.

On the numerous jaunts between California and Arkansas Clifford would spend part of each day grooming Fifi, and she depended totally on him for her beauty and apparently her well being. He would run through her coat with a metal comb to prevent the development of hairballs and tangles. He would also apply a special eye lotion to prevent her eyes from developing the eye discoloration that could be caused by the tearing associated with even half-Persian cats. When he was attending to Fifi, Clifford felt secure. He enjoyed the clear-cut rules of her grooming. His heart would sink in nostalgia and imagination as he listened to her purring in response to his attention. Any rage he had felt against his father or mother prior to the grooming process would dissipate in favor of an imaginative world filled with beautiful people, animals and luxury. Fifi served as Clifford's means of escape from his humdrum world.

During the family's many jaunts across the U.S., Clifford's anxiety would often return after he had groomed Fifi, and she had climbed back up behind the back seat of the car. He would suddenly awaken to his father's blathering about his last evangelistic campaign, his initial trip to California along Route 66 or his upcoming religious endeavors. Clifford attempted to block out the voice and the monologue but often was unable to do so. As the boring monologue continued, Clifford's anger and resentment grew.

During one early-summer trip in the 1950s, the family entered New Mexico, the Land of Enchantment, and the father unexpectedly announced he planned to stay in the state for at least two weeks. An acquaintance was attempting to establish a Jesus-only Pentecostal congregation in the town of Tucumcari to compete with the only Assemblies of God church in the area and felt the father's divine calling would prove beneficial.

Clifford heard his dad say that Tucumcari had originally been called Ragtown and then Six Shooter

Siding because of the numerous gunfights that broke out there. In the early 1900s, it briefly adopted the formal name of Douglas but changed its name to Tucumcari when it developed into a permanent settlement around 1908.

To Clifford, Tucumcari still represented its original name of Ragtown. He could find nothing of interest in the town and dreaded what he predicted would be hot weather. The area had a semi-arid climate characterized by cool winters and extremely dry, high-temperature summers. Thunderstorms with heavy downpours would be approaching within a few days. Clifford feared those storms and the extreme heat might imprison him in the inauspicious motel with only Fifi as his solace.

While the parents settled into the room in the practically-empty motel, Clifford talked with his mom about the times he would need to be in the motel for his school work. He wanted to plan something for himself.

"What time during the day would you like for us to sit together for my lessons?" Clifford asked his mom.

As usual, his mom didn't give a direct answer but responded with another question, "When would you prefer, morning or afternoon?"

Clifford thought for a minute and said, "Late afternoon might be best." By suggesting late in the day, Clifford thought, he might be able to have some time to himself.

Since the family traveled so much, Clifford could not comfortably enroll in a public school and succumbed to what was at the time a rather unusual learning arrangement: home schooling. Unfortunately, his mother was the teacher, but her personality did not lend itself well to successful teaching and learning. She had graduated from the University of Georgia with a degree in English Literature but had no imagination. She presented facts and requested that Clifford merely regurgitate those facts. Learning became a burden rather than a pleasant challenge for Clifford.

Once they had set the time for the class sessions, Clifford excused himself and began to research what tourist sites might be of interest to him. He soon discovered that the town boasted a dinosaur museum, a historical museum, a trading post, a mountain cheese factory and a movie theater. Outside the town limits was Lake Tucumcari, a reportedly beautiful body of water. The lake sounded very absorbing, and Clifford promised himself he would hike there the next day.

"Dad, I plan to go sightseeing tomorrow," Clifford said, assertively. "Don't worry about me. I'll be fine."

After all, he was twelve years of age and could take care of himself. His father viewed him rather suspiciously but said nothing. In fact, Clifford wasn't even sure his father had heard what he had just said. He was so engrossed in his sermon preparation and evangelistic operations that he temporarily let his control of Clifford relax. The mother, as usual, didn't seem to care one way or the other. She said only, "O.K., but be careful."

Clifford was particularly eager to have some time to himself prior to the beginning of his father's evangelistic campaign because he was quite sure his father wanted to draw him into the campaign activities. As they were approaching Tucumcari, his father had remarked that God had revealed to him that Clifford might have the gift of healing, and anytime that supposed gift became apparent or even if by accident a seeker was healed, the campaign crowd would grow exponentially. Clifford feared he would be presented to the attendees at the campaign as a divine healer with a direct connection to God whether he wanted to be or not, and he needed a little time to prepare himself for what he thought would be a debilitating moment. He wasn't sure he could stand up under the pressure.

The morning after the family's arrival in Tucumcari, Clifford rose early, made sure that Fifi was fed and groomed and slipped his knapsack on his back. Both parents were still in bed, the mother as quiet as a corpse, the father snoring so loudly that anyone listening might have thought he was having a "snore-gasm."

Clifford wrote his parents a note: "I have left to explore Tucumcari while the weather is cool." He closed the door to the room as quietly as he could and started out of the parking lot toward the street. He wasn't sure how far away Lake Tucumcari was, but he was certain he could hike there and back by late afternoon, thereby avoiding any unwanted fatherly repercussions or restriction to the room for several days.

154

He began his trek with his knapsack on his back. He walked for what seemed to be two hours in the direction he had been told led to the lake. By the end of the two hours he was sorry he had begun the hike. *What have I got myself into?* he wondered. He had been told he could take a bus but had thought some time alone in nature, no matter how bleak, would lift his spirits more than riding a bus for fifteen minutes, viewing a body of water for another fifteen to twenty minutes and returning to the town and his imposed incarceration in the motel room and its environs. He attempted to forget his tiredness and possible introduction as a faith healer by whistling tunes he could remember and thinking about a meal he might have on his return to the motel. But the strain on his back from carrying his knapsack and the pain in his feet from walking in shoes not actually made for long walks slowly turned his whistles into curses, for which he knew his father would reprimand him had he heard them. This was Clifford's first long hike, and he had not realized how much energy such a feat would take even a twelve-year-old.

Suddenly he spied a bus approaching, headed in the direction of the lake. He attempted to take his T-shirt from under his knapsack where he had hung it when he had begun to perspire badly in the New Mexico heat. He wanted to flag the bus down with the shirt, but it was so limp from the perspiration that it would only cling to his arm. His extremely white skin sparkled from the reflection of the sun on his sweaty body.

The bus looked particularly attractive because of the heat and Clifford's gradual realization that he had greatly miscalculated the distance from the motel to the lake. He wanted to take advantage of every second he had to himself that particular day before he had to face a crowd of expectant seekers of supernatural healing whom he feared would get angry when his gift of healing proved inactive or he was unable to meet their expectations.

The engine of the bus was in the front, the entrance in the back. A colorful banner covered the entire grill and sported a message printed in a language Clifford couldn't decipher. The message was intentionally coded since it was intended for members of the Apache Nation only. When translated, it read: "We are proud members of the Jicarilla Apache Nation and are bound for a spiritual weekend at Lake Tucumcari."

The dysphonic motor of the bus suggested poverty. The bus would every few seconds squirt black smoke from the exhaust with an explosive sound. The motor itself sounded like an alcoholic with a major attack of the hiccups.

The sides of the bus boasted multiple colors: black, red, green, blue, purple and white. Each color had significance for the tribal members and symbolized some dimension of tribal war paint. To Clifford, the many colors seemed more confusing than symbolic.

The roof was loaded to the hilt with suitcases, boxes and even a coop full of cackling hens. No roosters could be found among the fowls. These hens were intended to serve as sources of food rather than for reproduction.

The passengers themselves were chortling almost as loudly as the hens. They were excited to be nearing the lake, which for them had healing powers. Their excitement and noise increased significantly as they neared the destination to begin their planned spiritual retreat.

Clifford didn't realize that the occupants of the bus were tribal. He assumed they were merely poverty-stricken citizens of New Mexico attempting to do what he wanted to do: get away from the stress and strain of everyday life for a few hours. But as the bus drew nearer, Clifford realized it was transporting a contingent of tribal members.

The bus driver spied Clifford and stopped the vehicle only a few feet from where Clifford was standing. "What are you doing out here alone?" the driver asked. "Don't you know you shouldn't be near the lake without your parents or a companion?" He had immediately recognized that Clifford could not be more than twelve to fourteen years of age.

Clifford didn't respond immediately but approached the bus with reluctance and full attention. Would he want to board this vehicle with what to him was an unusual group of travelers, or would he opt to continue his journey alone? As he grew closer to the bus, he noticed that some of the male occupants wore beaded leather war shirts and boasted beaded bags with arrow quills. Other male passengers sported cotton tunics and

Mexican-style pants. A few of the men wore clothing that resembled the U.S. Army code of dress of the 1800s. The women had on simple calico dresses. Several wore their hair long and crowned their foreheads with red bandanas.

The entire group of passengers was a colorful bunch and quickly attracted Clifford's attention. His main hesitation to approach the bus focused on the question of the group's religious affiliation and beliefs. *Were they idol worshippers? Did they worship the True God or many gods? Would they attempt to take away his faith?*

These thoughts dominated his thinking for several minutes, but his curiosity finally overcame his reluctance, and he responded to the driver's questions. "I came from Tucumcari this morning. My parents are there in a motel, but I needed some time to myself. I wanted to see the lake but didn't realize it was so far from the motel where we are staying."

The bus driver, whose only piece of clothing that differed from the attire with which Clifford was familiar was his Apache T-shirt, stared at Clifford in disbelief. *This young twelve-to-fourteen-year-old boy is here alone,* he thought. *How could his parents be so foolish?* Without saying another word to Clifford, the driver reentered the bus and began a dialogue with several of the colorfully dressed tribal men.

After a few minutes, the driver again emerged from the bus and said to Clifford, "I have consulted with the Chief of the Tribe and several members of the Tribal Council, and they have agreed to invite you to finish your trek to the lake with us, and before dark, I will deliver you back to the motel in Tucumcari. We do not feel you should be alone out here."

Clifford reluctantly agreed to join them and climbed aboard the bus. His reluctance reflected his desire to be alone and his ignorance about the culture of the group that was befriending him, but his better judgment now told him that being a part of an organized team would be better than attempting to go it alone. Even though he knew his father was so occupied with and focused on the upcoming evangelistic campaign and that his mother would not complain about his extended absence if he were present at the time she had established for his tutoring sessions, he suddenly felt lonely and scared. Maybe he could see the lake and relax a bit with this group. They certainly seemed animated. Perhaps they could lift his spirits.

The driver seated Clifford next to him and began to talk with him as they drove toward the lake. "Where are you from?" the driver asked. "What are you doing in Tucumcari?"

"I come from California, but my father has agreed to work with a local Pentecostal pastor in setting up a church. We will be here for at least two weeks in an evangelistic campaign intended to attract locals to the new church through healing services and messages believed by my father to be directly from God for particular individuals and groups he feels need to find God."

"Interesting," said the driver. "Our group has come to Lake Tucumcari on a religious retreat, hoping for healings and refreshing of the spirit through bathing in the lake, listening to and watching our traditional Devil Dancers and laughing with the self-appointed clown. We are members of the Apache Indian Nation. Only three or four thousand of us remain. The rest have passed on."

The driver's statement both intrigued and frightened Clifford. He could easily relate to the idea of healings since his father emphasized that gift. But the words "Devil Dancers" made him shudder while, at the same time, piquing his curiosity. The Jesus-Only movement encouraged spiritual dancing in church, but that type of activity could be tolerated only when the dancer was assumed to be expressing himself/herself in worship. Anything having to do with the "devil" was to be avoided or purged from worship. Any individual thought to be under the influence of the "devil" could not be tolerated either in worship services or outside of worship. How could devil dancers not be devil worshipers?

Clifford finally summoned the courage to ask the driver, "Why do you have so few members of your tribe, and who are these Devil Dancers? Do they worship the devil?"

"Unfortunately, as I said earlier, the number of our tribe is decreasing fast," replied the driver. "And, no, the dancers don't worship the devil but are merely a part of our tradition. We believe that our ancestors existed alongside supernatural beings centuries ago. Even today we think spirits live in certain mountains and in areas underground. The dancers merely celebrate our tradition and beliefs. We don't think the dancers are of the devil but do think they can link us to our past through our imaginations and emotions."

After about ten minutes, the bus arrived at the spot on the lake that the tribe had reserved for their celebration. The riders emptied the bus quickly and prepared for their activities. They made themselves even more colorful than they had been in the bus. The Chief slowly got down from the bus and made his way to a spot central to all the activities. It was quite obvious he was the leader.

"How long will it be before the dancers perform?" Clifford asked the driver.

"They should begin dancing within the next half hour," the driver said. "Would you like to watch them? If so, I will try to get permission from the chief for you to stay beside me during the performance. I will ask the chief if I can take you home right after the show so that you won't be out after dark. I don't want your parents to become anxious."

"I can't let my parents get worried. If they do, my dad will be all over me," Clifford offered. "But I would very much like to see the Devil Dancers perform."

The driver disappeared for a few minutes, and when he returned, he said to Clifford, "The chief gave me permission to drive you to your motel in the bus right after the Devil Dancers perform. He has taken a liking to you. In fact, he has invited you to sit beside him during the devil dancing. That is quite an honor."

Clifford thought for a moment and then answered, "Just don't tell my dad I watched the Devil Dancers if you meet him when we go to the motel. He will think I have sinned and have become demon-possessed."

"Your dad is very religious, I take it," the driver said.

"Yes, he is, ridiculously so," Clifford agreed. "And if he thinks I have watched what he believes to be a performance of the dancers of the devil, he'll be totally freaked out. He'll not understand that the dancers are a part of your cultural tradition but will only see or hear the word 'devil' and punish me. Please don't tell him I sat with the chief and watched the dancers. I don't want to be made to stay in my room for several days."

"How old are you?" the driver asked.

"I am twelve but have lived a life that has made me very aware of the devil and his evil deeds," Clifford responded. "I talk like an adult because my father expects me to act like one and doesn't want me to be like a twelve-year-old. He has spiritual ambitions for me and wants me to avoid the devil and his evil works at all cost."

Just as Clifford was finishing his last sentence, the Devil Dancers appeared, and the driver introduced Clifford to Chief Nanoon, who greeted him with a wave of the hand and a motion to sit beside him. The driver retreated to the background.

Chief Nanoon had donned his headdress after arriving at the lake; the headdress bespoke of his bravery and power and clearly represented the culture of the Apache Nation. The headdress consisted of numerous feathers, each of which he had earned in an act of bravery. The collection of feathers included three of the most prized Golden Eagle feathers. Those feathers clearly demonstrated Chief Nanoon's outstanding loyalty, strength and endurance. His clothes consisted primarily of animal hides.

The dancers were eerie but magnificent-looking creatures. They sported wooden-slat headdresses and brandished wooden swords. They represented a defense against the tribal enemies and a protection from diseases. They supposedly had the power to summon mountain spirits. They served as a proverbial link between the supernatural and natural worlds and ensured the well being of the tribe. The dancers were not considered supernatural beings but did appear to possess "special abilities."

Chief Nonoon spoke English well and explained in a quiet voice the significance and background of the dances and explained that the dance ceremony generally occurred after dark. The exception was when the members of the tribe arrived at a place dedicated to worship and healing, and the lake was such a place. The arrival permitted the performance to take place in the afternoon. He was careful not to distract from the dancers' performance but seemed determined for Clifford to grasp the tribal traditions played out in the dances.

According to Chief Nonoon, the dances were adaptations of the Ghost Dance, which in turn, had evolved from a ritual common among tribes from pre-historic times. The dances represented part of the tribe's belief system and were intended to guarantee the reunion of the living and the dead and ensure peace, prosperity and unity among the tribesmen.

Most often only initiated men could take part in the dances. Those men didn't represent deities but were human beings with special abilities. Tribal men often honored the original Devil Dancers, who were believed to be invisible, by dressing in costumes with bells attached to the elbows, sleeves and leggings. These tribal look-alikes would hide behind bushes or trees until the actual dances had begun and would then run out, screaming and stomping their feet to the beat of the drums.

The dances often continued for days and required substitute dancers for those individuals who started the ritual. The dances could be very grueling. Observers responded to the dancers and dances, even the supposedly invisible dancers.

As Clifford watched the Devil Dancers, he tried to show little emotion, but his eyes widened, and his jaws tended to drop just a bit. The quiet but authoritative explanation Chief Nonoon offered of the dances intrigued him even more, and he began to ask the chief questions. "Do you believe in the devil? Have your beliefs remained pretty much the same for many generations? Are the Devil Dancers thought of as spirits? Why is there a clown among the dancers?"

Chief Nonoon listened carefully and attempted to answer each question as well as he could without becoming too technical about tribal traditions. "No, we don't believe in a devil as such but in evil spirits. Yes, our beliefs have remained pretty much the same for many, many years. No, the Devil Dancers are not considered spirits but are spiritual men, and the clown is intended to make people in the audience laugh."

Clifford's questions impressed Chief Nonoon very much. He could not remember having met another twelve-year-old boy as interested in what might be going on as Clifford.

A member of the tribe and apparent close confidante of Chief Nonoon set a full plate of food before Clifford and motioned for him to eat. Some of the offerings were foreign to Clifford's palate, but he tried his best to eat everything on the plate. The Indian-corn soup was delicious, but the dried eels and other boiled fish didn't prove very appealing. The young squashes and dumplings were only tolerable. Clifford ate heartily at first, not really thinking about the taste but only about pleasing the chief. But gradually he found himself nibbling as the dancers concluded their performance, hardly able to swallow some of the less-appealing dishes.

The performance came to an abrupt end with the clown approaching Clifford, making loud noises and falling down in front of him. Clifford didn't know how to react and continued to sit cross-legged. He didn't realize that the clown's prostration in front of him was a sign of respect and laughed only when the chief cracked a smile and motioned the clown to move on.

As soon as the clown got up from the ground the driver reappeared and suggested, "Clifford, don't you think it's time that I take you back to your motel? It's almost 4:00 p.m., and it will be getting dark soon. I don't want your parents to worry about you."

Chief Nonoon stood up and gave Clifford a big hug. "It has been a pleasure to meet you. I hope you enjoyed the dances and our conversation. I wish you the best," he said. He quietly told the driver to be careful on the way to Tucumcari. He certainly didn't want anything to happen to Clifford.

On the way back to Tucumcari, the driver told Clifford how much he had impressed Chief Nonoon. His eagerness to explore Lake Tucumcari, his willingness to experience the devil dances and his consumption of the different foods had inspired Chief Nonoon to exclaim, "This is an unusual young man. He is mature beyond his age. I like him very much."

Clifford was enjoying vicariously the adoration the chief had expressed concerning him and continued to be engaged in conversation with the driver as the bus approached the Tucumcari city limits. Suddenly, the driver exclaimed, "What's happening ahead?" The question hurled Clifford from his euphoria to reality.

In front of the bus were a number of cars. Each car was being searched thoroughly and each driver questioned. The bus driver and Clifford waited patiently until their turn, and when the police officer entered the bus, he asked, "Have you seen a boy about age twelve? He disappeared this morning, and his parents have not been able to locate him. They are very worried and have asked us to help them find him."

"What's the boy's name?" the driver asked.

"Clifford," the officer answered.

Clifford and the driver looked at each other, and Clifford reluctantly said, "I'm probably the boy you're looking for."

The officer looked at Clifford and then turned to the driver, "You are under arrest for child detention and possibly molestation. Anything you say may be used against you. Please follow me." The officer walked the driver toward the patrol car while removing from his belt a pair of handcuffs, which he forced on the driver's wrists.

Clifford wasn't sure what to do or say, but he did approach the police officer and said, "Officer, the driver has done nothing to me. In fact, he was extremely helpful. He picked me up on my way to Lake Tucumcari, made sure I was not alone at the lake and, with the permission of his tribal chief, brought me back to Tucumcari so that I wouldn't be late and worry my parents."

Clifford saw his parents and walked toward them. His father appeared ready to beat him, but Clifford knew nothing would happen until they got back to the motel.

He began to dread the wrath of his father's obvious anger but determined to help the driver get out of the mess he seemed to have created for him. He could see the puzzled look on the police officer's face but wasn't sure how to convince him of the bus driver's innocence and kindness.

Officer John Turlman suddenly realized he faced at least two major dilemmas. The first involved the possible questioning of Clifford; the second touched on interracial and intergovernmental relations. An officer had to be very careful when dealing with minors. One wrong move could cost him his job or create a lot of negative publicity, which would do neither him nor the police force any good. And the colorful banner covering the engine grill of the bus plus the numerous colors that graced the sides of the bus spoke of the Apache Indian Nation and a potential municipal-tribal conflict. He also feared Clifford's father might try to create a problem. He realized he had to watch his step, not vary even an inch from accepted legal procedures and use considerable diplomacy.

A fellow officer, Officer Brady, had become very aware of his mistakes in taking a minor into custody when he received a summons from a local judge to appear in court within three days after the minor's arrest. Officer Brady's appearance in court had brought a strong rebuke from the judge, who reminded him that a minor could not be viewed simply as a young adult. The judge had reprimanded Officer Brady for not reading the young boy his Miranda rights and placing him under arrest even though the boy had admitted to committing theft. The judge had informed the officer that not every minor had to be notified of his/her Miranda rights prior to questioning but stated that a situation involving a minor might trigger the notification of the rights more readily than one involving an adult. Officer Brady had definitely violated this particular minor's rights.

The judge had admonished Officer Brady in the future to consider carefully a minor's age before deciding to place a culprit under police custody and to use caution during the time of questioning. He emphasized the significance of Officer Turlman's mistake and suggested appropriate training and discipline.

As Officer Brady had left the courtroom, his cell phone had rung; when he had answered the call, he was instructed to go to the office of the chief of police. The instructions told him he was in trouble, and his intuition proved correct when the police chief informed him he had acted improperly for a police officer and would be suspended from his duties for a minimum of six months, during which time he was forbidden to participate in any police-related activity or make any statements about his suspension. He very worriedly spent his six months in semi-isolation and re-entered active duty with considerable trepidation.

The situation involving Clifford differed considerably from the case in which the thirteen-year-old had readily admitted to being a thief and the officer had been reprimanded, but the current situation could prove even more complicated than that of the fellow officer. *Was Clifford a runaway? Had the Apache tribe harbored a runaway even for an hour or so? Could the Apache tribe itself be considered at odds with New Mexico law by accepting and allowing Clifford to stay with them at the lake? Where would the chief fit into this picture? Could Clifford's father be cited for child abuse and negligence, prompting Clifford to leave his parents behind even for a brief period of time?* These questions haunted the officer as he pondered what to do.

The officer recalled that the update of the New Mexico Child Welfare Handbook stated runaway children could not be detained in secured settings while waiting for their parents. Neither could such children, according to the handbook, be readily taken into custody. Parental rights had to be given priority.

The revised handbook seemed to afford the officer a way out of the Clifford dilemma. He could and should refrain from detaining Clifford and should talk with Clifford only in his parents' presence. He would also ask a co-worker to be present throughout his discussion with Clifford and the parents.

The state of affairs related to the Apache Indian tribe presented a far more complicated and potentially ugly possibility. Officer Turlman's experience with the Apache Nation had been limited, but he knew the stakes could be very high and the consequences of a misstep great.

For many years, relations between the City of Tucumcari and the Jicarilla Apache Nation had been outstanding. City officials had respected the sovereignty of the Nation while the Nation had more or less followed Tucumcari's laws and regulations. But in recent years relations between the city and the nation had become strained, much less friendly.

The deterioration in relations between the City of Tucumcari and the Apache Nation had resulted from the arrest of a member of the nation by the Tucumcari Police Department without consulting with the Chief of the Nation and the Tribal Council. The chief had denounced the arrest and had stated in no uncertain terms that the city officials had exceeded their authority. He had admitted the tribesman had behaved incorrectly but had said the City of Tucumcari had no authority over a citizen of the Jicarilla Apache Nation. He had demanded the immediate release of the tribesman into his custody. It had taken two days for city officials to comply with the chief's demands, resulting in a further strain between the City of Tucumcari and the Jicarilla Apache Nation.

In thinking about how to maneuver his way successfully through the potential Clifford-Apache-Nation debacle, Officer Turlman assumed the driver of the much-decorated bus was himself a member of the Apache Nation and knew any actions taken against him would be viewed with suspicion by the chief and the Tribal Council. He did not want to be the cause or instigator of a further deterioration of relations between Tucumcari and the Indian Nation.

The potential diplomatic fiasco seemed further complicated by the presence of members of the nation at Lake Tucumcari. The agreement between the Jicarilla Apache Nation and the City of Tucumcari regarding Lake Tucumcari was tenuous at most and potentially explosive. The agreement gave the city authority over the lake but allowed the Indian Nation to visit and camp on the site as long as the tribal members adhered to the regulations imposed on other visitors by the Lake Authority and recognized by the city. As far as the Officer Turlman knew, there had been no infractions by the nation, but the nation's emphasis on the area as a sacred spot open to Devil Dancers and other Apache traditions didn't always bode well for improved Authority-City-Nation relations.

Within the nation, the seven-hundred-seventy–acre undeveloped reserve of which the lake and its surroundings were comprised represented a sacred area. The reserve provided excellent wildlife viewing of ducks, geese, golden eagles, doves, quail and pheasants. Members of the nation believed the hills surrounding the lake had served as the home of many of their ancestors and still held many ancestral spirits.

While the Jicarilla continued to be known for their pottery, basketry and beadwork, they enjoyed a substantial income from the oil and gas, casino gambling, forestry, ranching and tourism on their reservation. Any major hiccup in City-Nation relations could very easily have negative economic consequences for Tucumcari.

Officer Turlman knew both the mayor and the chief of police would be watching him carefully to see how he handled the Clifford and Apache situations; as he thought about the potential consequences of any mistakes on his part, his stomach churned. He was, he admitted to himself, facing the biggest challenges of his life and possibly the end of his career with the Tucumcari Police Force.

While Officer Turlman weighed his possibilities and considered his future, Clifford stood nearby, attempting to determine how to help the officer and approach his dad. He was particularly concerned about how to talk with his dad once they returned to the motel. *What would his dad have to say about his venture? Would his dad attempt to punish him for going out on his own and getting involved with the Apache Nation, which his dad undoubtedly considered devil worshippers?* After some time, he decided to forget about what might happen when he and his dad returned to the motel and concentrate on the situation at hand.

Officer Turlman suddenly had an "aha" moment and decided to throw caution to the wind. He would either become a local hero or an outcast for the remainder of his professional life. Perhaps getting Clifford, Clifford's dad, the bus driver and Chief Nonoon together could prove educational and diplomatically advantageous for everyone involved. The Chief of the Apache Nation would not look favorably on the retention of the Nation's bus driver. Clifford's dad was obviously upset not only with Clifford, but with the Indian Nation and the City of

Tucumcari for not putting Clifford in his custody without delay. The driver and Clifford were already present; he only needed Chief Nonoon. He immediately requested that the bus driver telephone the chief, inform him of the situation and tell him the Tucumcari police would pick him up within the next hour and bring him to the scene.

When Officer Turlman explained his plan to Clifford's dad, the dad objected under his breath but uttered no strong objections out loud. Clifford welcomed the suggestion, and the Chief of Police said nothing. The better judgment of the Chief told him the experiment would fail, and if it did, he knew he would have more than adequate reason to dismiss Officer Turlman. He was certain that violence would break out and a further rift between the Apaches and the citizens of Tucumcari would ensue. The bus driver just wanted to leave the situation behind and try to enjoy the short time he would be able to attend the Indian religious celebration.

Chief Nonoon flew into a rage when the bus driver telephoned him but did agree to come to the scene. He had been worried about his driver and wanted to make certain he was safe and free from the clutches of the Tucumcari police.

Officer Turlman dispatched a squad car to Lake Tucumcari to pick up Chief Nonoon, prepared a conference room in police headquarters for the group to meet and gathered Clifford's father, Clifford and the bus driver into the room. Nothing else could be done until Chief Nonoon arrived.

While waiting for Chief Nonoon to arrive, Clifford began to talk with the bus driver and quietly tell him how sorry he was that his act of kindness had resulted in the situation in which he now found himself. "I am truly sorry you are going through all of this just because you were kind enough to bring me back to Tucumcari so I wouldn't be late and my parents wouldn't worry," he said.

"You don't have to apologize," the driver replied. "None of this is your fault. You are a very nice young man, mature for your age. Both Chief Nonoon and I have enjoyed talking with you and getting to know you. You have really impressed Chief Nonoon."

Clifford also attempted to approach his dad, saying, "Dad, I am sorry to have created this problem for you. I know you have a lot to do in preparation for the evangelistic campaign that will begin within the next few days. Please forgive me."

His dad at first continued to ignore Clifford's comments and request for forgiveness, but slowly Clifford noticed a change in his demeanor. His face relaxed, and tears filled his eyes. He approached Clifford, said nothing, but opened his arms, seemingly inviting Clifford to be embraced. Clifford obliged, and the two hugged each other for several minutes without the exchange of a single word.

After some thirty minutes, Chief Nonoon arrived, accompanied by two of the highly decorated Devil Dancers. As soon as he entered the conference room, the Chief went straight to Clifford and gave him a big hug.

Then he said, "The Dancers insisted on coming with me. You impressed them so much with your attention and apparent interest in our culture that they felt a kinship to you almost immediately and wanted to make certain you were safe and happy."

Clifford didn't know exactly what to say but was finally able to utter, "Thank you, Chief. Thank you, dancers. I liked your performance and really enjoyed learning that being a 'Devil Dancer' did not mean you were worshipping the devil but merely paying tribute to your culture."

Clifford's father raised his eyebrows in apparent surprise and concern over his son's statement, but before he could say anything, the Devil Dancers were in front of him, bragging about Clifford and his mature approach to life. The father thanked them for the compliment and said little more.

The atmosphere was tense for several minutes in the conference room, but the Apache Chief eventually said, "For his diligence and professionalism, I would like to thank Officer Turlman, who discovered Clifford and the driver and kept them safe. I would also like to thank the Chief of Police for showing respect for our Nation by allowing the squad car to pick us up and bring us here. We had no means of transportation except the bus. This courtesy lets me know that the City of Tucumcari does not bear animosity toward our Apache Nation and does want to enter into an era of peace and cooperation."

The Chief of Police shook Chief Nonoon's hand and quietly introduced him to the mayor, whom the Police Chief had secretly notified of the Indian Chief's presence. The mayor shook Chief Nonoon's hand and said, "The City of Tucumcari would like to enjoy excellent relations with the Apache Nation. After all, we are residents of the same area."

"Thank you," Chief Nonoon uttered. "It is my pleasure to meet you and get to know you."

The formal greetings turned into lively conversations, which continued for more than an hour. Finally, Officer Turlman announced that the Tucumcari City Council was scheduled to meet in the conference room where they were within the hour, and the unscheduled gathering would unfortunately have to end within the next half hour.

Without any fanfare, the Apache Chief raised his hand and announced, "I would like to pay honor to Clifford. He has been able to do something for the Apache nation and Tucumcari that no Indian tribesman or municipal officer has been able to accomplish. He has brought us together. Thank you, Clifford."

"I would also like to thank Officer Turlman for his courage. He took a huge chance, which could have backfired and put him in a very difficult position. But his intuition proved correct. Thank you, Officer Turlman."

The members of the group clapped for several minutes, shook hands vigorously and finally had to say goodbye. The bus driver hugged Clifford, and Clifford clung to the driver as if he were his savior. Clifford's father for the first time in Clifford's recollection smiled at Clifford and patted him gently on the head. No one left unhappy.

When they arrived back at the motel, Clifford's father proudly told the mother about Clifford's diplomacy and said, "I am proud of our son. In his own way he has already evangelized Tucumcari."

Clifford didn't know how really to respond but merely said, "Thank you, Dad." He hugged both of his parents for several minutes and then went to check on Fifi and quietly explain the day's happenings to her. Fifi merely rubbed against Clifford and purred rather loudly.

Clifford's father continued his preparation for the evangelistic campaign but said nothing further to Clifford about having to participate in the campaign as a faith healer. A week after the informal meeting in the conference room, both Clifford and his parents were asked to appear before the Tucumcari City Council where Clifford was awarded a Certificate of Recognition for his accomplishments in bringing the Apache Nation and the City of Tucumcari together for the first time in many years.

The award created an immediate reputation for Clifford and prompted many Tucumcari citizens to visit the motel as well as his dad's evangelistic campaign. The campaign continued for some two weeks and boasted a crowd of several hundred each night. Much of the talk before and after the nightly services was about Clifford.

Many attendees shook Clifford's hand and congratulated him on his accomplishment.

Each night, Clifford's dad seemed to have developed a greater respect for him and even mentioned him several times during the sermons. But nothing was ever brought up about Clifford participating in healing services. Apparently, Clifford had done enough to more than please his dad.

Officer Turlman also received a Certificate of Recognition the same night that Clifford was honored, and within a month after accepting his certificate, he was promoted to captain of the police force. Neither the mayor nor the Chief of Police could say enough good things about him. He was the talk of the town and dubbed a hometown hero by the local newspaper.

Gradually, Clifford's relationship with his father improved, something he never expected on that long, dusty trip. And, ironically, it was the Devil Dancers that he had to thank for that.

Cecilia Pugh

Cecilia Pugh, a Northern California native, received her B.S. degree from San Jose State University and is an Occupational Therapist specializing in geriatrics. She is a poet, a writer of both fiction and non-fiction, and a member of California Writer's Club Mt. Diablo Branch.

Cecilia's country roots and her love of humanity—coupled with her strong spirituality and endless curiosity—have made her an astute observer of the human condition. As a widowed mother of four children and a grandmother to five, she has experienced many of the joys and sorrows of life.

All of this is reflected in her literary work.

Cemetery Hill

We were close enough to hear the loud cannon explosions and the roar of muskets as the two sides faced off at Cemetery Hill. My mama, younger sister, brother and I, were hunkered down in our small log cabin hoping the Confederate soldiers would be contained by the Union Army. News of the Civil War and the advancement of General Robert E. Lee's men heading north would trickle in as men on horseback passed through our town heading for large gatherings of Union soldiers positioned beyond Gettysburg.

I was only twelve when my daddy signed up to fight in the Union Army. I offered to go with him to help load his musket, 'cause my daddy had taught me how to shoot and kill rabbits. I still remember what he said, and how he looked at me with a faraway look in his eyes and only one side of his mouth turned up in a half smile.

"Son, I want you to stay home and take care of your mama while I'm gone. You need to do your share of chores, tend to the fields, and fish and hunt to feed the family. Life will get harder after I'm gone. You're the oldest, and I'm counting on you. Someday you will understand, son, that a man has to stand for something and fight for what he thinks is right."

He looked handsome as he mounted our mare named Betsy dressed in his navy-blue uniform, high black boots, and brimmed cap that covered his dark wavy hair. Mama kept a brave face until he was out of sight, then she dashed into the house, buried her face in her apron and sobbed.

Times were tough. When daddy was off fighting my mama never knew where he was or if he was okay. It had been a long year without any word if he was alive or dead. We were expecting the worst as we heard stories about recent battles that had been won by General Lee's Confederate Army.

One day I was returning from the river. I'd caught six fish, and I couldn't wait to show them to my mama. As I got closer to the house I saw a horse tied to the fence and recognized Betsy. The sight of her gave my heart a fright, and made my knees want to buckle out from under me, 'cause the last time I saw Betsy, Daddy was riding her away to join the Union Army. I dropped my fishing pole and the fish, and ran as fast as I could to the house. When I opened the door my daddy was holding my mama in his arms and she was sobbing into his chest. My sister and brother had ahold of each one of his legs. I screamed "Daddy, Daddy, Daddy," over and over and ran up and threw my arms around him. He stayed long enough to give us a hug and kiss and tell us how much he loved us before he had to leave and report to General Meade near Cemetery Hill. He said they were expecting a fierce battle, but Daddy felt the Union Army would be successful, as he believed in General Meade's skills as a leader. His last words were, "I will be back when the battle is over." I close my eyes and return to that day over and over again.

When the roaring of the muskets and cannons had ceased, a strange sound drifted from the field. It started out as a low moaning and slowly escalated as more voices joined in crying for their loved ones, as they lay dying. Day after day, we could see and hear the wooden carts filled with dead and wounded soldiers pass by our house. My eyes will never let me forget what I witnessed, nor my nostrils the stench of death. Mama wouldn't let me go check to see if Daddy was okay.

"He will come when he is able to let us know he is okay, just like he said."

We had heard General Meade's Union Army was successful and General Lee and his surviving soldiers were retreating to the south. My family was expecting to see Daddy show up on Betsy like he did before the battle started. One day someone knocked on our door. When my mama opened it there were two men dressed in blue standing as if at attention in a parade.

"Mrs. Jackson, we are sorry to have to give you the bad news. Your husband Bill Jackson was killed in the battle at Cemetery Hill. His body has been buried in a mass grave outside of town. We thought your son would want to have his bayonet and hat."

My mother took the hat and bayonet and slowly shut the door. She leaned against the door and collapsed onto the floor. My brother and sister grabbed onto my mama and started wailing. I stood there in disbelief like a wooden statue unable to move, as my eyes burrowed into the floor in front of my feet. When I saw my mama reach out with her arms I knew she was okay, so I bolted. I ran as fast and as far as I could through the fields screaming, "No!" at the top of my lungs. When I finally stopped to catch my breath I fell face down and pounded the dirt with my fists. Then the words my daddy spoke to me flooded my mind: "Son, I'm counting on you." Slowly I walked back home, grabbed my fishing pole and headed out toward the river to catch some fish for dinner so we'd have something to eat.

Four months had passed since the death of my daddy, and the town was getting ready to hear President Abe Lincoln give a speech at Cemetery Hill dedicating the field in honor of those who lost their lives defending the North. I have been there often, walking the battlefield trying to imagine where my daddy stood defending his beliefs. Dried caked-on red stains mixed with grass and dark earth covered every inch of the field. If I stayed silent, the wind told me stories about the brave men of blue and grey who stood on opposing sides of the field, tall and proud, strengthened by contrary views that sliced a deep gash separating the North and South just as this battlefield had done. Each one was prepared to give all, convinced his side was right.

I pictured them lined up shoulder to shoulder, marching forward one foot in front of the other as each walked toward death's door. The screams that escaped their mouths must have hidden the fear that trembled within their souls. I heard the boom of cannons explode around me and I remembered the bodies on the carts with flesh hanging from their bones. Forever advancing, stopping only to reload a musket or position a bayonet. Kill or be killed. Honor drove them onward until they were forced to rest horizontally, as death took them into her grasp; their bodies now the quiet protest.

My mama, sister, brother and I had been at Cemetery Hill for nearly an hour waiting for President Lincoln to arrive. Finally a group of men on horseback showed up near a white tent placed on the field, and someone yelled, "It's President Lincoln."

President Lincoln removed his hat and walked over to a raised area on the field and began speaking. This was the first time I had ever cast my eyes on our President and from where we were standing I could only see his face and shoulders. He was taller than most men, lanky, not broad shouldered, and his posture was bent as he leaned over to read his speech. I didn't know how old he was but he had lots of deep lines in his face, a large forehead and nose, sunken eyes and a dark beard, making his face look long and weary like a sad dog that hadn't eaten for a long time and had given up asking for food.

President Lincoln's speech lasted only a few minutes, but it is one I will never forget. His words made me proud of my daddy and those who fought at his side to assure that all men would be equal and have the same guaranteed rights. He said we should honor the dead, never forget what they did here and continue the cause.

As I looked around me I could see young and old alike sobbing during his speech. And my own tears, that I had been hiding from my mama so she would not worry, poured out like a waterfall. I didn't have to hide anymore behind my pretend grown-up-mask. I could release those tears and cry like a little boy hurting for his daddy. It was a moment of healing for me, and for the large group of mourners whose grief was so evident for those who shed their lifeblood beneath our feet.

I imagined my daddy's arms around me, and somehow on that day I felt we answered with our tears of love, the last moaning pleas uttered by those dying soldiers at Cemetery Hill.

From My Window

❦

I was blessed with a loving family, an oddity in the slums of the South Side of Chicago. My mama was a teacher and concert pianist, and my daddy a janitor who dreamed of being a doctor but did not have money to pay for his education. Despite what I encountered every day when I left our second-story apartment to go to school, I knew I would come home to love.

Mama walked me to school when I attended grammar school because she taught the third grade. When I started high school I walked to school alone keeping my head down not looking at anyone so I wouldn't draw attention to myself. I tried to avoid approaching or looking closely at people in the streets who were sleeping under cardboard, alcoholics in drunken stupors, and people dying from lack of shelter and medical help. It wasn't that I was numb to the pain, because it cut deep into my soul like a knife, but I knew the only way I could cope was to express my sorrow in a poem.

As more people moved into the slums and extended families sought shelter, it felt like our apartment building would burst at the seams. People lingered in dimly-lit hallways trying to escape for a moment from cramped living spaces. Poorly insulated walls between the apartments exposed the verbal anguish of living in the slums. I could hear the wailings of restless hungry children with rumbling empty bellies trying to fall asleep; loud arguments that escalated and ended in harsh thuds and crashing sounds as families living together in one apartment tried to resolve their frustrations. There were nightly alcohol-induced ramblings of our neighbor next door as he downed cheap wine to numb the anger and sorrow in his heart, after his wife left him for another man.

Because I was shy, non-athletic, and had a fancy name, "Gwendolyn," my schoolmates rejected me. When they went off to play without me, I sat down with my pen and paper and retreated inwardly to my safe place where I could freely express my feelings. I developed a love of reading when my mama took me to the library. I would sit for hours lost in the pages of a story as the words transported me beyond the slums and filled my head with dreams. She and daddy read to me often when I was young, and always praised whatever I wrote.

My mama used to pound away on the old beat up piano she got from the church just like she was telling a story. She loved rhythm and blues and the notes got real loud when things were troubled and soft and tender when she felt God touching her. The vibrations would sink into my brain talking to me of messages about love, hate, sorrow, poverty and regret. She never spoke those thoughts; she let the keys talk for her.

My daddy worked every day of his life, resigned to pushing a broom instead of healing folks like he wanted. Somehow he turned a negative into a positive so his family would benefit. Daddy wasn't a bitter man. He knew he had to have a job to support his family and being a janitor provided a steady income. He always demonstrated an inner strength, never grumbling when times got bad. He would just dig in and resolve problems and help others in the process. I learned a lot about sacrifice and true love from him. I think down deep he was rightly proud of me when I published my first poem in a children's magazine when I was thirteen.

For a while in the 1930s, I went to an all-black school. Because my skin was light and my hair wasn't tightly curled, they thought I was a mixed breed and rejected me. When I transferred to an integrated high school I came face to face with high and mighty white kids. I put up with taunts, pushing and shoving, telling me where to sit, when it was okay to speak, and how I could be in their sight by not existing.

"Shut up. Be quiet. Don't cause problems. Move out of the way. Sit at the back of the bus."

For a while when I was young I followed their rules and kept a low profile, but I looked and listened and wrote down my observations as poems. I tried to turn the noise off in my head, the battles between my pride and others who thought less of me because of my darkened skin.

Whose dictionary did a better job of defining values, character, or pretty? Theirs or mine? Pretty was in their white egg-shell colored skin, yellow hair, and sky-blue eyes. Look over here! I'm a person too—and pretty. My skin is golden honey brown, my eyes and hair jet black like the midnight sky. I bleed like you do, see what you see, feel pain, hunger, love. Inside me runs a river, a torrent of emotion swirling with hurricane force just waiting to push and recklessly toss about anything in its path. Its only chance for calm is the writing pen, the magic wand that rips up the paper, expressing silently the words I want to speak aloud.

I tried to think of different ways to take away my anger so I didn't lose my pride and feel like a trapped animal in a cage with no choices. Each day to trick my mind into a peacefulness, I set a goal to find a simple victory that would be unnoticed by my white classmates. Like being the first black girl at the end of the line of white classmates going into the school lunchroom. I'd place a poem on the teacher's desk and she read them to the class with other stories without using my name. The students thought she was reading poems from some famous poet. Sometimes I'd smile quietly to myself when a streak of sun came in the classroom window and rested only on my shoulder, like God was telling me all was okay because He loved me. Most times the victory was a new poem crafted about the happenings of the day.

When I ran out of material to write my poems, I just looked out the corner window of our two-story apartment down onto the streets of the slums. There were people with tattered clothing begging for food, and sleeping and dying on the streets. We didn't have much to spare because our family struggled to put food on the table but my parents did what they could to help others. Women wearing bright red lipstick walked the streets, getting in and out of beat-up cars and walking to nearby rundown cheap hotels in the arms of fancier dressed men. Kids played with deflated balls, threw rocks, jumped rope, and drew outlines in the dirt of the streets. Sometimes there was loud screaming and fights as drunken men placed their bets on the two men who were fighting. Men hung about in groups selling and passing drug hits in exchange for hard-earned cash.

The streets, where an impoverished humanity existed, fed me literary treasures for my poems. For a short time I could hide away in our apartment, my pretend castle high above the ruckus and devastation, as I looked down on all the hurt. Deep inside the pit of my stomach, I felt a raging battle going on. And then the poetic rambling in my mind began to word paint describing my feelings, and I couldn't write fast enough to keep up. I never knew from where my inspiration would come.

Once, on my way to school, I rounded a blind corner and to my horror realized I was directly behind the same group of boys who, a month ago, had chased me home after school because I was walking on the same side of the street. They promised to beat me up if that happened again. If Mr. Sloan, a rather large man with a menacing face who lived in my apartment building had not been walking down the street, they might have succeeded. All the kids in my neighborhood were afraid of Mr. Sloan and would make up stories about how he got the scar that sliced through his right eye and across his lips and jaw making him scary looking, and blind in one eye. Mr. Sloan just stopped in the middle of the sidewalk, stared at the boys and growled. They looked at one another and ran the opposite way. I was frozen in my tracks not knowing what to do, and he just winked at me with his one good eye and said, "Have a good day little missy." Now I smile and wave at him whenever I see him.

This time my protector, Mr. Sloan, was nowhere in sight and the boys began to call me names, as they remembered I was that same girl they had chased. They came up close surrounding me and I got a sick feeling in my stomach like I wanted to throw up. I could feel my heart pounding so hard in my chest as it tried to escape. Some kids were looking around nervously to see if anyone was watching, when one of the older kids shoved me hard knocking me down under a bush next to the road. They pulled my hair and kicked dirt into my face before they ran away laughing. I started to get angry, as tears of resentment burst from my eyes. When I stood up and got myself under control, a flutter of movement in the bush caught my attention. I saw a cluster of green cocoons that were split open with brand-new butterflies hanging on the bottom, fanning their colorful wings like they were testing them for flight. It was like some sort of message telling me I wouldn't always be trapped like a caterpillar in a cocoon; I could become a beautiful butterfly. The butterflies became a symbol of hope for escape beyond my pain and anger to a happier place. Words, like an

African drum beating in my soul, flew out of my mouth and I, Gwendolyn, wrote this poem:

Fly Away

The cocoon is empty
nothing will return.
Water cascades over the rocks
the sun embraces the mountain
a new day awaits.
Her face is not familiar
she wears a new dress.
Let the celebration begin,
the present has been unwrapped
and beauty created,
taking flight into the unknown.

Much time has passed since a frightened young girl saw hope in the fluttering of butterfly wings. Poetry became my passion and focus, allowing me to be bold and confident when expressing feelings. My words became a golden ticket that transported me away from the slums of Chicago into the national spotlight, as the first black woman to receive a Pulitzer Prize for poetry. I escaped from pain and anger transformed into a beautiful butterfly who emerged from a dark cocoon of prejudice, to fly away into the sunrise of a new day.

Let the celebration begin!

To honor and give tribute to Gwendolyn Elizabeth Brooks (1917–2000), who inspired this fictional story.
She won the Pulitzer Prize for Poetry in 1950 and was appointed Poet Laureate of Illinois in 1968 and Poet Laureate Consultant in Poetry to the Library of Congress in 1985.

Table Number Fifty

❖

Suzanne prepared for this night as if she were taking a final exam, rehearsing in her mind how she would gasp in surprise when Paul pulled out the small box, and got down on one knee to propose.

For years she was secretary of his law firm, date for all social events, best friend and confidant. Paul never forgot her birthday, and always gave her flowers and unique gifts that demonstrated his caring. At social events she loved how he wrapped his arms around her when she shivered, held her close when they hugged goodnight, and the way his eyes lingered as he approved a new outfit she wore. He seemed to make excuses to come into her office so he could visit with her, appearing genuinely interested in her life. When he was not having lunch with a client they would walk to their favorite Italian restaurant to watch the owner throw dough until it was the right circumference and munch on vegetarian pizza. They both loved the hustle and bustle of nightlife in a big city and after working long hours would go to dinner and a play. She often described her job as, "the dream job," because it was more fun than work. And then with a twinkle in her eye would say, "Because I get to be with Paul."

Girlfriends tried to arrange dates for her with their brothers, but she kept her time free to be available whenever Paul needed her. His life was chaotic and he worked long hours to become a successful attorney.

Her first clue their relationship was moving from *secretary* to *girlfriend* had been six months ago when he invited her to go on a three-week cruise to Mexico. The trip would include a mix of business, involving three days when they first arrived, and the rest of the time he assured her would be theirs to enjoy. She was thrilled and looked forward to spending time alone with Paul without the interference of a demanding work schedule. Just a few days before the scheduled trip, Suzanne had to cancel because her mother had a stroke. Paul was disappointed, but assured her there would be opportunities for another trip in the near future. Before he left, he seemed distracted, staring at the wall with the same furrowed brow he displayed when reading an important brief. When she asked him if he was all right he responded, "I just need a long vacation to get away from this business." After he was gone for a few days, she knew he was relaxing when he stopped calling to request that she set up future appointments.

He returned home rested, unencumbered by a burdensome workload. His face glowed, and his body was tanned from the warm sun. He seemed to have a new lease on life, a renewed energy. He would come into the office, put his arm around Suzanne's waist and dance with her around the room as he hummed show tunes. For several months he was more playful, almost giddy, like a kid with a new bicycle. He asked her personal questions related to having children, the type of home she would want to live in, and furniture that she liked, which made her hopeful of a future with him.

He ordered a cab to pick her up to take her to an elegant restaurant as he had a last-minute meeting with an important client before their scheduled dinner. When she arrived, the waiter dressed in a white jacket took her directly to table number fifty. The table, designed for privacy, was tucked away into a corner, and known only to the waiters as *honeymoon haven*. Many girls had received proposals, and the waiters collected high tips for being respectful and discrete, leaving a couple alone to enjoy romantic time together.

Suzanne sat waiting for Paul to show up poised in her floor-length blue strapless evening gown that shimmered in the golden glow and flickering of candles that adorned the small table for two. A slit up the side of the gown revealed long, slender legs, like those of a model. Her dark hair was arranged on top of her head in a unique twist, which left bare her willowy neck where designer jewels cascaded down her comely chest and sparkled like stars from her petite ears.

Like a video camera recording a documentary her eyes surveyed the table setting: the red-velvet roses in a clear-crystal vase, bottle of Chardonnay wet with moisture from chilling nearby in a bucket of ice, the soft-light from the candles reflecting on the polished silver candelabrum. Her finger traced the raised Baroque pattern on her sterling silver fork and the delicate rose petal design that encircled her bread plate. She wanted to etch each detail of this special night into her brain so she would never forget.

The vivid memory of that night flashed into her mind again as the cab pulled up in front of the restaurant and a greeter opened the door offering his hand to assist her out of the cab. Like clockwork she arrived every April 22nd at seven o'clock and sat at her requested table, number fifty, in the back corner of the restaurant. Her request was always the same, a glass of Chardonnay, the chef's special hors d'oeuvre, white candles in a sterling-silver candelabrum and red roses in a clear vase. For many years her ritual went unnoticed, just another single lady waiting for her man to arrive. She became a legend when the owner began to recognize her voice and honored her requests. Among the waiters she was known as, *the lady in blue* because she was always elegantly dressed in the same blue strapless gown: her hair in a bouffant style on top of her head, on her ears and neck the same sparkling jewelry she wore the first time she came to the restaurant.

Gradually, over time, her hair changed with the style of the times and began to gray. There were noticeable dark sunken areas under her eyes, a vacant blank stare from her lackluster blue eyes. Flats replaced the three-inch black heels. The hem of her dress was altered, the slit sewed shut, and straps added to keep the dress from falling down. A black shawl for warmth caressed her bony shoulders.

Sam, a twenty-year employee at the restaurant showed her to the table and greeted her with, "Evening, Ms. Suzanne, I trust you've been well. So good to see you again."

"Good evening, Sam. May I have two glasses of Chardonnay? I'm celebrating a special occasion tonight."

"Very good, Ms. Suzanne, I'll be right back with your wine."

She glanced at the table. Everything was in order, the roses, white candles in a sterling-silver candelabrum, Baroque silverware, and the same bone-china pattern with rose-pedals. *Everything the way he had ordered it that night fifty years ago.* And she had been faithful to him, coming as he had invited on the special hand-written invitation, now framed and hanging on the wall in her home.

I love you beyond all telling
You are the air that I breathe
The beat of my heart
My universe, my strength, my everything.
If you feel the same, would you honor me
With your presence on _____
Elegant Turtle Restaurant
Table number fifty
All my love,
Paul

Sam interrupted her thoughts when he arrived with two glasses of Chardonnay.

"How many years have you been coming here Ms. Suzanne?"

"Fifty years tonight, Sam. It's our anniversary."

"Is that how long you were married?" Her smiling face changed to one with deep furrowed brows. "I was never married," she admitted.

"Ms. Suzanne will he . . . will you be having company tonight?"

"Sit down Sam, I'm going to tell you my story." Sam responded slowly, first taking a glance around the room and then at his watch.

"I only have a few minutes, Ms. Suzanne."

"Paul," she began, "had one last meeting before coming to meet me, and it turns out that is exactly what it would be . . . his last. A disgruntled client ended his life with a bullet to his heart."

"Oh . . . oh Ms. Suzanne, I'm so sorry, how dreadfully sad for you. But... you are still coming . . ."

"They found the ring . . . right there in his coat pocket, a large solitary diamond, along with a love letter he wanted to recite. Yes . . . the love letter was right there next to that beautiful ring. I remember going with him to the jewelry store . . . he thought he was being discrete by casually asking, "If a man were to propose to you, which ring out of this section would you choose?"

"I forgave him because I thought he wanted to make sure I really liked the ring he wanted to give me."

She stopped a moment to take a long sip of her wine, staring deep into the glass as if retrieving a buried treasure. Then she sighed . . . a long deliberate sigh like one would make when trying to rid the body of all

200

impurities. And then a gasping sob that began deep in her throat emerged and was followed by several sobbing sounds as her body shook back and forth.

Sam reached out and gently touched her shoulder. "Ms. Suzanne, you don't have to continue. This is too much . . . losing what appears to have been the love of your life." She lifted her head slowly and stared at him with wide-open eyes. Her ivory make-up and rouge was streaked by rivulets of tears that mixed with black mascara and ran down her cheeks, filling the hollows under her eyes and wrinkles that accentuated her pale lips, giving her a ghostly appearance.

"The letter was his own," she began slowly, as if enunciating clearly so a child could understand. "He never asked for suggestions to write a love letter. I wrote all of his letters, but this one was his own . . . from his tender heart." She began to sob again.

Sam stood up and looked around trying to get another waiter's attention.

"Thank you for sharing your story with me, Ms. Suzanne. Let me get you some Kleenex, I'll be right back."

"No Sam . . . don't leave me. I want to tell you . . . I need to tell someone." Sam slowly sat down again with a concerned look on his face that portrayed deep compassion. He looked up to see another server glancing in his direction. He gave her the restaurant's coded sign, a circling index finger, which clued the other server to 'take over, I have a problem at my table.'

"It was unlike Paul not to call and let me know he was going to be late. After forty-five minutes I got worried and took a cab back to the office expecting to see him still engaged in his meeting, and forgetful of the time. Instead, I found him . . ." She began to sob again. "I found him slumped over his desk with a pool of blood at his feet. I became hysterical and ran screaming and crying to the evening Security Guard who called the police. I wanted to die right along with him that night. His family and law partner made all the funeral arrangements and let me know the time and place for the service. Mourners packed the church and I sat down in front behind his family.

When asked if I would like to give a eulogy, I declined knowing I would become too emotional. His older brother Bill stood up first and shared funny memories about when they were young. Then his law partner got up to speak about more recent memories. He began by sharing stories of their friendship, and experiences as law partners. With frequent hesitations and a quivering voice that exposed his sorrow, he explained that Paul had recently fallen in love and was in the process of preparing to ask the love of his life to marry him.

"Sam, I began to feel myself shake all over and I didn't think I could suppress the loud sobs that were forming in my throat. Fortunately, I was not the only one having difficulty, as many family members were crying loudly and hugging one another. His partner paused a few moments, as if trying to swallow tears. He wiped his eyes a few times and then continued. 'I have permission from the family to read you the beautiful love letter he wrote.' As he began, I could feel myself get light-headed and I thought I might faint. This was more than I could tolerate. I didn't think any other person was aware of his love for me. I decided to stay put, because to get up and leave would create a spectacle, and disrupt the funeral. He began to read, 'to the love of my life . . . Madeline.'

He continued reading but I didn't hear a word he said. I was in shock. Madeline was the sister of his best friend and law partner. In the pew directly in front of me someone put an arm around her and was stroking her shoulder as she leaned in sobbing on his chest. The revelation that it was not I whom he loved felt like being hit in the face with a baseball bat.

He only wanted me to meet him here to approve the restaurant, table number fifty, and the invitation and love letter he had written to Madeline. I had the invitation because he left it on top of a pile of briefs that he asked me to pick up from his desk about a week before our scheduled dinner. Of course, I assumed the invitation was for me, but I did wonder why he never filled in the date. I thought it was just because he was busy and forgot. I never knew he had a personal life beyond our impromptu dates or business events. Apparently he wanted to keep the potential engagement a secret from his family, until she accepted. I found out later that Madeline made a last-minute decision to go on the cruise, using the ticket that was meant for me.

Tears began to roll down her checks again and Sam handed her a cloth napkin from the table.

"Ms. Suzanne, thank you for sharing. That was not an easy story to tell, and must have been difficult for you to retrieve painful memories."

"You must be wondering why I still come to this restaurant every year." Before he could answer she continued, "I lost someone I deeply loved and even though he didn't love me in the same way, he brought great happiness into my life, a happiness I have not been able to duplicate. It is my way of honoring his memory. For one evening a year, I can pretend I am still waiting for my lover."

When Sam stood up to leave he noticed several other waiters standing in the background, wiping their eyes. They nodded respectfully, code for time to get back to work, and slowly left. Sam reached over and gave Ms. Suzanne a long friendly hug, and excused himself.

As they watched her slowly shuffle past them to exit the restaurant, Sam spoke softly to the other waiters, "I wonder if we will ever see Ms. Suzanne again?" They continued their conversation in quiet jubilation, like detectives who had cracked open a cold case, solving the mystery of *the woman in blue,* yet mournful about the tragic ending.

Ms. Suzanne was an important part of this restaurant, like the pillars that kept it upright. Indeed, if Ms. Suzanne, a woman with deep passion, did not return, she would be missed just like a favorite aunt who had died. It was the patrons after all, who brought the restaurant to life, filling the dining room with laughter and celebration. Its walls held their secrets, rejoiced with each promotion, acknowledged personal accomplishments, suffered with their sorrows. They were the ones who made it become a living organism, breathing in and out, alive with the affairs of life.

Hog Maws, Chittlins 'n Pig's Feet

❧

I done some horrible things in my lifetime. That's why they locked me up 'n tossed the key into the Mississippi. I used to catch walleye, catfish, 'n baby gators in them waters. I'd just a soon fish than do anything else. We was poor white folk, and when I were a young'n thought I'd be a famous cook. Had a hankerin for makin weird food to freak out all my friends. They come back for more so guess I were pretty good. Used my Grannie's cornmeal 'n beer batter recipe to coat walleye and any creepin creatures I could find, then deep fry um 'til they was golden brown. Made sure I had hot sauce for flavorin 'n lots of cheap beer to drown out them flames. Weren't 'til they finished the fish 'n critters that I told um 'bout what they just ate. After them eyes got big, 'n them faces turned gray, they darted off to retch.

Been in here so long don't know what real food tastes like; it all looks the same, 'n tastes like marsh slime flavored wif puke. It's only ten days 'til my execution, 'n guards are callin me "the walkin dead." We're s'pose to feel all goose bumpy thankful that we get to order one last meal of our favorite food. Ain't that great? Wonder if we can order out.

My mind keeps wanderin back to them good old days in Nawlins when a bunch of hongre folk gathered 'round Grannie's table to devour all the fixins. Each plate were heaped high, spoutin steam and smellin of grease, jest beggin to be ate. She lived in a shanty shack so close to the water if you tripped off the back porch you'd be swimmin. I learnt all I needed to know 'bout secret ingredients—stuff she used in her favorite recipes—from watchin her after Mama started leavin me there, when I were only four. Sometimes I'd stay for months before Mama come back. Then one day, she jest disappeared.

Grannie had good reason to be mad at life, but she weren't. Grampa left her jest after her only child, my Mama were born, 'n she had to figure out how to survive. When Mama didn't return, she jest kept goin on, like nuttin happened.

"Don't never be bitter 'bout life, cause it rips open yer heart," she'd say.

Anythin creepin on the ground, flyin in the air, or livin in them waters could be ate. It jest had to be catched. 'Cause I were always hongre I learnt real quick how to chase, hold down, 'n knockout my food. Got real good at sling-shottin to take down them marsh hens, 'n had no gumptions 'bout sacrificin a fat worm on the end of my fishin hook. Sometimes I'd catch smaller fish 'n cut off a hunk of flesh to lure them hard to get catfish, the ones big a 'nuff to feed ten folks I reckon.

At age five jest to show I were tuff I went with Grannie to them slaughterin houses. Thought I might spill my guts the first time they slopped some them innards into my bucket. Grannie were always first in line to get them chittlins, hog maws, ears 'n feet. Folks in them parts

207

put her up on some sorta throne, seein how she were the best cook fer miles, 'n she didn't fuss any when folks needed a meal. I reckon that's why they was always bringin her stuff to add to the pot.

Next to her shack were a makeshift shed with a dirt floor what were used to keep that extra food. I liked goin in there jest to take a wiff of them smells. She had rows of garlic 'n onions on strings, branches of bay leaves 'n hot red peppers hangin to dry, piles of potatoes jest sittin on the cool earth, 'n rows of canned tomatoes jest beggin to be ate. We had buckets full of salt 'n beans, twenty-pound sacks of flour 'n cornmeal, baskets of eggs, jugs of cider vinegar 'n homemade whiskey 'n beer, which I weren't s'pose to touch 'cept on special occasions. When she weren't hangin headless chickens to let blood drip out before puttin um in boilin water makin it easier for me to pluck them feathers, I'd hang out wiffin 'n dreamin 'bout her food.

When we got home from them slaughterin houses Grannie went straight to fixin a big meal. She needed my help to drag out them big iron pots, fill um with water, 'n get a fire started under that outdoor stove. When the water were good 'n hot she added pigs feet, hog maws, 'n chittlins. Next I member her addin pinto beans she soaked all night long. When we was cookin, Grannie never stopped givin me lessons on life.

"Sonny." That's what she always called me. "Yer heart can never be too full of love fer folks. Always help um 'n don't 'spect nuttin back. Some folks is slow to let love blossom, kinda like pinto beans. You jest put a couple of hands full of beans in the bottom of the pot to boil 'n after a few hours them beans swell up real big, fillin up the pot. A little is a lot dependin on how yer lookin at life. God gave us everythin we need to survive we jest gotta share it wif love, 'n not get greedy."

Then come onions, tomatoes, hunks of bell pepper, a handful of garlic 'n red peppers wif seeds, a scoop of salt, 'n peppercorns. After that she turned a jar of cider vinegar upside down and poured a nuff 'til she were satisfied. Next come beer the part I liked 'cause she always poured 'bout a quarter cup for the two of us to savor whiles we was fixin the meal. And last of all no matter what she were fixin she always had a secret ingredient. In the beginnin she didn't let me get too close to see as she waved her arms over the food droppin this 'n that whiles she mouthed words like some sort of magic chant I reckon. Then we went inside 'n made cornbread wif fresh eggs, thick milk, cut corn from them cobs, spoons of sugar, handfuls of flour 'n cornmeal, 'n a hunk of fat, scooped up from last nites dinner. Like always, she added that final secret ingredient.

Folks jest started gatherin 'bout the same time when they got a hankerin by the intoxicatin smell, the food were ready. All's Grannie had to do were to leave that stirrin spoon in the pot, 'cause they came wif bowl 'n spoon in hand. She jest sat back in her rockin chair wif that all knowin smile glowin like she won first prize. Them folks had the same reaction as me after taken the first bite. Wif closed eyes we lifted them prayerful lookin faces toward the sky 'n sighed a thankful sigh. It were hard to know what to eat first, her butter-slathered cornbread, or dig a finger into the bowl fer them juicy pigs feet to suck on. Folks here was used to spicy, the hotter the better. Food needed to be so peppery hot that seconds into the first bite yer eyes got real big, face turned beet red, 'n drinkin a jug of water weren't a 'nuff to slow the burnin. Seemed like our tongues needed to be in flames to appreciate the food.

Sometimes on Sundays Grannie would add my favorite fried dough dessert, the beignet. She made um Saturday nite 'cause them had to have time to puff up. Then she added that special ingredient as she dropped um in boilin fat for 2-3 minutes. When they was cool 'nuff, like some sort of fairy blessin them mounds of joy, she would put her special blend of lite snowy sugar, cinnamon 'n nutmeg on the top. Them smelt like I imagined heaven to smell. Grannie always said, "Heaven smells sweeter than dogwood blossoms. It's a place where we're hugged by love so pure, we ain't gonna want nuttin else." I always slit um open 'n added a spoon of honey that made my mouth get watery, 'n my throat sing as that honey slid slowly, from my mouth to my stomach.

Folks always got real quiet when they was eatin, kinda like somethin sacred was goin down, 'n only folks in attendance was havin this experience.

Grannie died when I were jest eighteen, the only family I ever had, 'n I fell apart. Missed her somethin fierce so I ran away, drank too much 'n holded up the bank when I were too drunk to care. They said I kilt someone but don't member nuttin. I sobered up real quick when them guards threw me in a cell wif bars, 'n shackled my feet to the bed. I felt trapped jest like them animals I catched fer food. It were more than a country boy from Nawlins could take. Thought I would be dead in a week. But I hung onto life thinkin 'bout how tuff Grannie were 'n how much she loved me. She'd want me to be tuff, so I jest closed my eyes 'n made believe I were back in them woods climbin up to my secret place, a flowerin dogwood tree, wif thick scruffy weeds 'n vines hangin on them branches to hide me whiles I were huntin. I felt the cool Mississippi waters runnin over my toes like when I fished fer catfish. Heard the oo-wah-hoo-hoo call of mournin doves singin them songs of lament, 'n stared down gators glidin smooth cross them waters wif black eyes peerin straight at me tryin to see who were the scaredy cat. Didn't think 'bout them trapped animals, jest 'bout bein free.

In prison I had plenty of time to think 'bout that secret ingredient 'cause jest fore Grannie died she told me the secret. When I were re-born at a religious service here at the prison I shared that secret so utter folks would be blessed. It were this prayer, "Jesus, fill up them empty spaces in them hearts wif yo love." Plain, simple, 'n powerful, jest like Grannie.

My mind began to drift off 'n I thought 'bout my execution. I heard Grannie say, "Me, Saint Michael 'n his helper, are comin to take you to heaven."

A voice shook me back to reality, "What do you want for your last meal son?"

I smiled my best smile, 'n wif all honesty, 'n straight focused eyes like I were stockin prey I whispered, "Nothin thanks, my Grannie's fixin a meal; she's been spectin me."

Waiting In Line

Salty droplets of sweat pour down his furrowed brow making his eyebrows glisten and his dark eyes blink. He can't use his hands to wipe because they are encased in mandatory plastic gloves required by the Health Department when one prepares or serves food to the public. He grasps a large handful of grated cheese to sprinkle on the pile of rice, beans, sour cream and chicken before grabbing the edges of the flour tortilla and wrapping the mound into a tight edible cocoon known on the menu as, 'The Big One.'

I'm hoping drops of his sweat don't fall onto my burrito, and am estimating what might happen first. Either the sweat falls into someone's food, or he flexes his right arm and wipes his brow on the sleeve of his new white t-shirt that has the company logo printed on the front. It's a beautiful girl with long flowing black hair wearing a large flower behind her ear and a bright red dress. You tend to notice things like that while standing in a long line with nothing to do. It's a forced observation time to keep the brain engaged. I'm betting on a salty droplet being added to someone's order.

It's mid-day at the Memorial Day Festival in Grant's Pass, Oregon, and I'm one of twenty people waiting to state my request for food at the Rosita Canteen. Most of us seem patient, but I imagine like me they are dreaming of sitting in a tub of ice in an air-conditioned room. I'm trying to decide if I really want to stay in this line, so I take a quick survey of the food vendors and realize they all have long lines.

The young couple in front of me is trying to lock lips and he is being particularly cautious about where to place his lips as she is wearing a diamond studded lip ring that seems centered in the fatty part of her lower lip. I turn toward my left side trying not to stare in disbelief or notice their public display of affection, but I'm curious about the ring in her lip. I think it must hurt a little. Both have added hot pink hair spray to their heads. His covers the raised Mohawk strip from his forehead to the base of his neck and she has a long pink ponytail twisted loosely on the top of her head. She is wearing a sleeveless shell, lime green in color with a flowered print, and I'm not sure where her clothing ends and her tattoos begin. They are both wearing torn jeans and I can see slivers of white flesh exposed through the openings. Worn saddle-brown leather boots complete the outfit.

He's probably six feet tall with bulging biceps and broad shoulders, maybe an ex-football player. His tattoos look like a Native American Indian design, with a dark solid leaf-like pattern that crisscrosses and goes up both arms from his forearm to the crest of his shoulders. They are both young, maybe twenty-one or two. Then I hear a baby cry and I realize these two young ones in front of me are pushing a stroller. The baby's cry gets louder and people are glancing their way so the woman finally tears herself away from locking lips and picks up the infant. I remind myself that I was also young when I had my first child. Once she is holding the baby they are both making sweet cooing sounds. The baby is wearing a hot pink bow that compliments the mother's hair and is clipped onto a large tuft of black hair that looks like they might have used gel to make it stand straight up. I even say a few words like, "You have an adorable baby."

She smiles and says, "Thank you. Her name is Daisy, and we almost lost her at birth because she came prematurely and had to stay at the hospital for three months before we got to bring her home."

"How old is she now," I inquire.

"Five months old today."

The dad takes the baby and places her across his chest, cradling her with a wide-open palm, snuggling Daisy's head on his shoulder and into the side of his neck. He is making rocking motions and kissing her cheek and Daisy begins to quiet down. He looks like a gentle giant.

"You have the magic touch," I murmur.

"I was the oldest in my family and I took care of all of my younger brothers and sisters so my mom could go to work after my dad died."

The part of me that doesn't trust strangers expects more sob stories and an eventual request for assistance. Fortunately, the sensible and emotional part of me wins out and I am blown away by someone who learned responsibility at an early stage in his life and demonstrated an unexpected tenderness.

"Sounds like you have lots of experience parenting."

"He's a perfect dad," she says, looking at him with glowing eyes.

I smile and think *there are treasures everywhere; one just has to look.* And I remind myself, *never judge a book by its cover.*

My thoughts are interrupted by the guy with the sweaty brow who is asking the gentle giant what he wants to order.

He responds, "Two chicken burritos with extra salsa, two bags of chips, and two large Pepsi's."

"May I buy your lunch?" I hear myself saying. "I think your mama would want me to. To thank you for all that you did to help her."

The gentle giant looks at me with wide eyes and a serious expression on his face. He turns away for a brief moment and when he glances back I can see tears forming in his eyes.

"My mama died unexpectedly last month in her sleep. It means a lot to me that you would say she would want to thank me. It's . . . it's like she's standing right here telling me." Now the three of us get misty-eyed and a young girl helping the man with the sweaty brow and white t-shirt with the company logo looks at us and says, "That will be twenty-four dollars."

As I hand her the money the couple give me a hug and say, "Thank you so much," before leaving with their order. I look over at the guy with the sweaty brow who is bending his head and lifting his right arm to wipe his forehead on the sleeve of his new white t-shirt with the company logo.

I breathe a sigh of relief and say, "One chicken burrito with everything."

Carlos de Jalisco

Carlos de Jalisco escaped the sweatshops of Florida in the late 1960s and found a home in labor-friendly California.

He writes because, "It's fun," requires only pencil and paper, and doesn't consign him to debtors' prison, as would hobbies like yachting or Formula One racing.

He gets inspiration from classes and strange events, but generally writes whatever pops into his little mind. Nobody confuses his work with literature.

Carlos now lives in Northern California.

Thrill Hill

❧

Thrill Hill was never a hill. It was always a bridge, the South Avenue Bridge. It provided a way for vehicles to cross Dixon's Ditch, a canal that flowed glacially into the bay a half mile to the east and didn't smell too good. It spanned no more than sixty feet but what separated it from other bridges of its length was a sharp rise to a crest of twelve feet, not only making it one of the highest elevations in the state of Florida, but creating a safety hazard as it blocked the view of the road on the other side from all motorists who didn't have X-ray vision. It was that crest that put the thrill in Thrill Hill.

The city traffic bureau made sure motorists got the message. At least two blocks away on either side, signs with flashing amber lights screamed, "Reduce Speed Ahead, Narrow Bridge, Limited Visibility, Speed Limit 15 m.p.h., Strict Enforcement." If English was the problem, reflectors coated with fluorescent amber shone in drivers' eyes to alert them of the impending changes. For those who still didn't get it, the confiscatory fine levied in court settled the issue.

Motorists had long ago made the scientific discovery that when they hit the bridge at faster than some minimum velocity, whether through negligence or premeditation, the vehicle went airborne after the apex, creating that weightless, free fall, stomach-in-mouth feeling as the vehicle descended on the other side. Ongoing trials proved that the higher the velocity, the further the flight, and the greater the ecstasy.

"It gives me a sensation I didn't believe existed," said one high school chick whose eyes appeared permanently crossed from the experience. Another compared it to sex! "I can't tell the difference," she moaned. It was like Six Flags Magic Mountain and Disneyland without the price of admission and long lines. On Friday and Saturday night, Thrill Hill became the Mecca for teenage motorists and thrill seekers from miles around—a sideshow, 1960s style.

Not all sensations at Thrill Hill were sexual in nature. The head-ons provided some wild spectator value. Vehicles hit the cement culverts and posts at either end of the bridge and finished second best in those collisions. And since seat belts were not required in those days, drivers played human dart—the last thing that went through their minds was the windshield. Auto interiors and the surrounding asphalt got a fresh coat of red paint.

Ambulances, fire engines and the jaws-of-life became frequent visitors to the Hill. When the carnage reached threshold levels the cops got visible again and lined both sides of South Avenue with motorists pulled over for speeding, reckless driving, and the occasional drunk. In response, infractions—and accidents—almost disappeared. The cops whose efforts had brought things under control withdrew in phases and went back downtown to arrest jay-walkers. Thrill seekers scared away by the cops slowly came back to the Hill and the cycle, which lasted about three months, started again.

The local newspaper weighed in regularly about the meat grinder on South Avenue near Clay Street. Editorial commentary appeared in local newspapers imploring the city to demolish the crested bridge and replace it with a flat one. Neither newspaper nor lobbying efforts of citizens carried the vote. It would take something more.

"More" came down one Saturday night when three teenagers in a supercharged Pontiac GTO hit the bridge at, just say, over the speed limit and sailed off. Imagine their "thrill" when, while in flight, they discovered the taxi that was parked just on the other side. Even state-of-the-art brakes couldn't stop an airborne vehicle.

The picture on the front page of next morning's paper said it all. It depicted the GTO with its front axle on the cab's back window, the underbelly on the trunk, and rear bumper resting on the bridge behind the cab. The muscle car had "mounted" the taxi, if you will. The inescapable image of two dogs in love was the talk of that city for weeks; only it took more than a bucket of ice water to separate the vehicles. Miracle of miracles, no one got more than a few scratches, but the resale value of the cars took a hit and the cab driver lost his license and did time after blowing a .24.

The caption under the picture read, "When, If Not Now?" That jarred the city officials and within two months the "Hill" had been replaced with a flat bridge that allowed unlimited visibility on both sides. Accidents ceased. No more sick concertos of blaring horns followed by screeching tires, percussive impacts, twisting metal, shattering glass, and sirens. The jaws-of-life never showed its molars again. Teenagers went back to Disneyland and Magic Mountain. The thrill was gone.

Ice-Breaker

⚫

Mother Innocentia, principal of St. Isabel's, led her entourage—fifteen nuns, citadels of chastity, clad in their black and white finery, crucifix and beads rattling from their cinctures. They took seats in a special section of the auditorium, sequestered from the unwashed like a jury, although I wouldn't have wanted any of them on *my* jury. I saw one new face and it was *not* Mother Theresa and remembered the rest from the previous eight years and how they terrorized every student in the school. Dan Digby and I were happy to be just visitors on this day.

"Public school kids don't need this," I told Digby. "They just go to the dance."

When the nuns had taken their place, Mother Innocentia took the podium and addressed the hundred or so freshmen boys and girls who jammed the auditorium for the orientation session on the eve of our first high school dance—the Ice Breaker. We called the session, "dog obedience school."

"Welcome, students. Today, we will instruct you as to the code of conduct that you will observe tomorrow night. You've heard it all before, just behave as you have been taught in religion class, only now your actions will have greater consequences."

"I'm surprised they let boys and girls under the same roof," I said.

It's about time," said Digby. "But I still think they're worried about scandal."

Catholic administrators had a decade earlier separated genders in their schools. "Children learn better and mature faster without the distraction of the opposite sex," they claimed, so they stuck boys in one end of the schoolhouse, girls in the other. In the church, the cafeteria, the auditorium and the gym, it was boys on one side, girls on the other, " . . . and you don't even look at the other side," ordered the nuns. A glass curtain bisected the campus and they even tried to extend it off campus. Teachers forbade students from going into Porky's, a soda-jerk place across the street from school because of its party atmosphere.

"It's the devil's workshop," the nuns said, "and we know who goes in there."

After eighth grade, the boys escaped to St. Anthony's High School where priests ran the show, leaving the girls at St. Isabel's with the nuns.

"I really pity the girls," Digby said. "They have four more years in the 14th Century."

"They'll probably fit us for straight jackets at the door tomorrow night," I said.

Although the big dance would be our first in high school, many of us had partied for the previous two years and gone to monthly cotillions, semi-formal affairs sponsored by the city, where we learned basic dance steps along with decorum appropriate for mixed company. Our school administration condemned these events.

"It's way too early. We don't need our children dating at age twelve and getting married at age fifteen."

They tried to prevent us from joining. Priests and nuns threatened and cajoled, but almost a full roster of our class attended these dances.

Mother Superior continued. "At this time I would like to introduce Sister David Mary who will conduct the session. Sister David is new to our school but has years of experience organizing social events like this. Sister!"

Sister David Mary walked to the stage. A shadow fell over the room. She eclipsed everything in her hemisphere and seemed to burst out of her size 6XL habit.

"Whew, she's a big one," Digby observed.

Big Dave looked capable of picking up the podium and throwing it a long way. She tapped the microphone twice and uttered "testing, testing" several octaves lower than bass, adding to the mirth in our corner of the auditorium.

"It doesn't surprise me that she took a man's name," I said.

"I think she wanted 'Butch,'" Digby said, "but somebody beat her to it."

"Good morning, students," boomed from the podium with enough decibels to render the speaker system unnecessary. "I hope The Ice-Breaker tomorrow night will be conducted with full awareness on your part of the mystical body of Christ."

Leave it to the clergy. Whenever the situation called for specifics, they ran and hid behind some fuzzy doctrine that not even *they* understood.

"I have chaperoned public school dances in the past and have been taken aback by the lewdness and licentiousness in the dance hall. The place turned into a den of iniquity. Much better will be expected of you. While dancing, you will observe a respectful, moral distance between you and your partner. The Sisters and I don't want to spend the evening separating couples."

Murmurs rumbled through the boys' side of the room like a fast freight train. Some of us did the unspeakable and looked across the aisle where the girls were grinning. Sister David stopped and glared in our direction, silencing the chatter.

"I can't believe that's the same bunch that we grew up with," Digby whispered. "They got some real lookers over there."

"Ya know," I said, "we could deplete the cache of plenary indulgences that we've saved over the last eight years at one three-hour dance. Tomorrow night could be more fun than I ever dreamed."

David shot us a hard glare then continued. "You are at an age where your bodies are changing and new temptations will test you. We all go through that every day—sins of the flesh. It is an easy path to follow, to give in to your pleasure instincts and let the animal in you take over. At those times you must pray, 'Satan, get thee away from me!' Girls, the boys will be right there to entice you.

They are *not* on your side. They only want one thing, and it's not something you want to give them. It's always on their mind. I know boys and I know men, so be on your guard."

The women in the black and white glared in our direction. Some of the girls who were grinning earlier now eyed us with suspicion.

"Look at Rosie," Digby said.

Sister Marie Rose, who had taught us in eighth grade, sat in the gallery burning Digby and me with two laser beams. In religion class she had this obsession with the Sixth Commandment. As if timed by God, actor Errol Flynn—the Brad Pitt of his era—died that year of "unspecified causes," giving Rosie unlimited grist for her daily lecture.

"Unspecified causes? Ha! He died of a social disease," she pounded, over and over.

"I remember," I said. "She turned crimson and breathed so heavy that if Errol Flynn walked in that room, he would have had her hot enough to fry eggs on."

"In conclusion," said Sister David Mary, "I just want to say that our bodies are not objects of pleasure. They are temples of the Holy Ghost and you will treat them as such. So come to the dance tomorrow night and have a blast but don't forget the mystical body of Christ."

"Hey Danny . . . triple dare you to ask David Mary to dance tomorrow night. I'll bet you don't have the guts."

"I've always liked athletic women," he said, "and she *does* look like an East German luge driver. I'll tell you what, you ask Rosie and I'll ask Dave—we'll make it a foursome!"

The dance promised to be an interesting duel between God's Law and Natural Law, Mother Superior vs. Mother Nature, religion vs. science. Pubescent girls erupting with estrogen, and pubescent boys teeming with testosterone, would seek to deploy their natural talents, restrained by fifteen militantly celibate women—could be an untenable situation, like driving a race car with one foot on the accelerator and the other on the brake at the same time.

Outside the gym the next night, we could hear 45s being spun by some local disc jockey with strains of Elvis, the Shirelles, Bobby Darin and the Everly Brothers cranked at full volume. We paid the fifty-cent tariff and went in, only to be confronted by a sea of black and white. I thought at first that Sister David Mary had called for backup but I was just paranoid. For at least a half hour, chaperones outnumbered the dancers.

Old habits died hard as in the early going, the kids observed the girls-on-one-side, boys-on-the-other doctrine until the disc jockey announced, "This is a dance, not solemn high mass," and played some Elvis hits to prove it. Finally, the two groups mixed and soon the place turned into rush hour as even nerds and geeks grabbed partners and hit the dance floor.

Fast dances ruled, we guessed, as ordered by our chaperones, frustrating the instincts of those who would get familiar. The nerds and geeks danced far enough from their partners that you could have driven the Pope-mobile between them. But most of the kids who had experienced the adoring touch of the opposite sex gave Sister David and her Gestapo all they could handle when the music slowed. Nuns observed from the perimeter, eyes peeled for lewd behavior like an Elvis hip gyration. Then they came right out on the dance floor and circulated among the couples, looking for evidence of pleasure.

When the disc jockey played "Are You Lonesome Tonight," Elvis's all time best seller, swoons escaped from the females. Partners got closer and closer, wrapping both arms around each other so they looked like one person with two heads and four legs. Some stopped all motion, eyes closed, and didn't really dance at all, they just stood there rubbing bodies. Ears and necks became targets for hot breath and nibbling teeth. Pulse and breath rates climbed.

The black and whites went on high alert. Surveillance and enforcement increased. When they spotted a couple having too much fun, they stood and glared, most often at the girl and let Catholic guilt do the rest. For most close encounters, they acted like referees at a boxing match, separating fighters locked in a clench.

"You two, Adam and Eve, back up . . . leave room between you for your guardian angels." The Mystical Body of Christ was nowhere to be found.

Their tactics did manage to throw ice water on some raging fires, thwarting some momentum at least temporarily. The nuns won the battle, but Mother Nature won the war. Some, like Digby, managed to elude the guards and danced close without interruption. He had bragged at the orientation, "If Dave and her deputies want to separate me and my girlfriend they'd better bring crowbars and a fire hose." Meanwhile, busted couples simply postponed their interaction until the long walk home under a full moon.

Dancing in the heat brought out the sweat in everyone, all of whom had applied way too much perfume or cologne, which commingled and transferred to whatever hot body they came up against. Slow dances gave each person the summation of all partners' fragrances he or she had acquired during the evening. At the end of the dance, everybody smelled like everybody else and the gym smelled like a French brothel.

Our little foursome with Rosie and Dave never materialized. "Good thing," said Digby. "I think both of them had sensitive trip wires and we didn't want to provoke their animals."

Take the same chaperones and put them at a high school dance in 2014. By then they'd be in their early 130s, but still living in the 14th century. How do you suppose they'd react as they circulated among the nubile couples but instead of having to separate Adam and Eve, now they had to separate Adam and Steve?

Pavlov's Revenge

◆

"Aah!" I purr, when I hear that familiar whine. "It's the electric can opener." I'm like Pavlov's cat. In fact, my master named me 'Pavlov.' When I hear that thing I salivate whether she is doing Spam for her boyfriend of the month or Purina scientific designer diet for me. I hustle into the kitchen.

"Look who's here," she said. "Must be free food! You and my boyfriend never turned down anything free, so now, one of you has to go. I can't support both of you plus two kids on food stamps alone."

Ten years earlier, just after she yanked me out of a dumpster where we were fighting over the same food, she got knocked up twice, once each by two different low-lifes and both did the honorable thing and jammed for the exits, bringing bad pub to a gender that didn't need it. After the second one bolted, *I* got the trip to the vet.

Why me? She should take her boyfriends to the vet.

"I'm going to make a responsible young man out of you, Pavlov," she said. The vet did his thing. I still haven't recovered either physically or psychologically and it's been a decade. There is no justice. Humans can have us fixed but they're the ones that need fixing!

The real fathers should have stayed because they don't know what they missed. The two little girls they sired turned my life around. I'd much rather play with them than have to tolerate the scum that continues to pass through our revolving door. None of them had jobs but they all shared their own versions of the American dream, their pie in the sky, their sure thing. One bragged that, "I'm just about to score the most incredible job." Another said, "I'm just about to score that giant drug deal in the sky." Yet another, "I got the six winning numbers in this Saturday's Power Ball Lottery." She fell for every one! The due date of the promises came and went without delivery, but hangers-on still hung on for at least another year. The current stiff, my competition, milked us for two years in the dream of a multi-million dollar insurance settlement that would deliver us to Utopia.

"Then it's you and me on easy street, doll!" he told my master over and over.

I've done everything I could to warn her about these chumps, and I have called every one of them. I've sounded my high-pitched squeal when they walked in the door. I've jumped on their heads and tried to scratch their eyes out. I've even pissed on their legs, but she just doesn't get it. What do I have to do, go upside her head? Do I hear 'bum magnet?'

After a streak of losers, she actually brought home a nice guy one evening. He leaned down and petted me and said, "Hi, Pavlov. I've heard a lot about you."

He reached into his pocket and pulled out a gourmet snack for me. It smelled expensive. I scarfed it - the most incredible taste treat of my life.

My God, I thought. *A class act: her ship just came in.*

They sat on the sofa and I eavesdropped from the space in between them. He had a job and owned a *house.* Imagine that! He said it had two stories, a yard, trees to climb. I pictured us there. I nuzzled his leg. He picked me up and put me on his lap. I stared up at him, sending the message to my master, "Don't let this guy out of here without a marriage proposal." She missed that one, too. Soon, he was gone and the vacuum filled by the current shitball who promptly got his eardrums pierced, his eyes scratched out, and his leg pissed on like a fire hydrant.

So, on selection day, me and fat boy drew straws. I drew the short one and stayed. And it was only right, I guess. I had a better resume since he spent his days on the computer playing video games and listening to Rush Limbaugh all the while dipping into cold pizza, ice cream, and Jack Daniels—his three major food groups.

In fact, I'm the only one here who pulls his weight. I babysit her two little girls who think I'm adorable but the time commitment threatens my sixteen-hour-a-day sleep regimen. I provide security with my high pitch squeals, which, by the way, went up a few octaves after my trip to the vet. Then I help the whole housing project by supplying mouse and rat control, natural and organic— I guess you could say "green." No need for harmful chemicals, traps, or firearms, just the food chain! I could live very well on the rodents of this project, further proof that people need us more than we need people!

Meanwhile, she keeps the place paw-deep in torn up lottery tickets and the junk she buys "at a steal" from some flea market. The most recent purchase drew my attention as I peeked over the edge of the box. A vibrator and a lamp? I could understand the vibrator because it had more personality and it provides her with more utility than her boyfriends.

"The merchant said the lamp was special," she claimed.

Then I see something weird going on with the lamp. It's like a cloud escaping and forming a genie. I squeal and jump nearly to the ceiling. My master comes running in and sees the thing.

The genie tells my master, "You've had a tough life. I will grant you any three wishes." I hold my breath.

She looks around. "I wish this project be turned into a mansion in the Napa Valley." Poof! My master, the kids, and I suddenly stood on a hacienda balcony overlooking fifty acres of cabernet grapes. "You have two more," said the genie. "Choose wisely!"

She thinks and thinks. "I wish to go into a time machine and relive my life starting at age twenty-one as a drop-dead beautiful starlet." Poof! There appeared in my master's place a cross between Angelina Jolie and Halle Barry—made me wish I were human!

"You have one more wish," said the genie. "Make it count."

She thought longer and harder than she had for the first two wishes. Then she looked at *me*. I covered my head. "I've got it! Transform that old alley cat into beefcake with the bronze tan and rippling physique who just walked off Muscle Beach in Venice." Poof! There I stood in my Speedos with a body that would have shamed Arnold at his most steroid enhanced.

Looks like I got my wish. My stunning master clutched at me, tore at my flesh, moaned, unable to catch her breath.

"I have to have you, right now!" she gasped. I started to laugh.

"Did I say something funny?"

"Kind of! I'll bet right now you're sorry you took me to the vet ten years ago."

Night of the Dragon

❖

The throaty exhaust of the Ford 4x4 heralded the arrival of Jo Beth Lester's parents, Billy Bob and Roxana, from work. Jo Beth stood in her garden and watched as her father backed his baby into the driveway. "Always easier to back in than back out," he liked to say. "And it's easier to unload after our trips to WalMart."

Jo Beth had an unobstructed rear view of the black monster—the gun rack, the dog box, the whip antenna, and those bumper stickers. One read, "Pro Life," the other, "Gun Control Means Hitting Your Target." A burnt orange silhouette of a steer's head with horns that spanned the width of the tailgate, dominated the back of the pick-up. A redundant "Hook 'em Horns" appeared beneath it.

Billy Bob, a truck driver in Crawford, Texas, and deacon at First Baptist, and Roxana, a grade school teacher, had told Jo Beth that they wanted a decision about college no later than the day after she graduated high school. They had definite plans for her future based on their priorities in life: God, family, and tradition. A four-year degree in education from the university in Austin, then a career back in Crawford "teachin' l'il school children," clashed with Jo Beth's plans. She had made it clear that she wanted to major in theater at Juilliard in New York City and to pursue a career on stage.

Even though both schools had accepted her, the contest between Texas and education vs. Juilliard and theater defined the relationship between Jo Beth and her parents throughout high school. Roxana and Billy Bob had indulged their daughter's fantasies to a point but cautioned her not to get too serious about theater. Now that high school had drawn to a close, they would be telling her that the curtain had also come down on her acting career.

The night before, Jo Beth had taken her high school stage for the last time and delivered a rousing valedictory address that challenged her classmates to "throw off the chains of conformity and forge your own way." She didn't stop there. "Girls, it's up to our generation: let us exercise our reproductive freedoms." And, " . . . explode those glass ceilings. The workplace belongs to us, too."

Billy Bob and Roxana had to dodge the flak thrown at them by friends and neighbors at a graduation party. "Your daughter git that shit from you, Billy Bob?" And, "What's Jo Beth smokin' these days?"

The couple piled out of the truck, hugged their daughter and all three headed for the house. Once inside, Billy Bob made a beeline to the fridge where he secured a tall one of ice cold Pearl Beer "from the country of 1100 springs." Today, he had something to celebrate. After mortification the night before, Billy Bob wasted no time redeeming himself. This morning, he achieved local rock star status when he called a nationally syndicated talk show—and the call was answered! Friends and colleagues heard him greet the host with, "Mega dittos from Crawford, Rush!" before he asked, "Men is marryin' men out in California, ain't they?" The host had just finished his favorite commercial, the one where he boasted that his show claimed "the most educated audience of all nationally syndicated talk shows."

Billy Bob joined Jo Beth and Roxana in the family room and sprawled on his recliner as he popped the frosty cylinder of Pearl. He took a hit as though he would inhale the whole can.

"Wow!" he said, after swallowing. Jo Beth rolled her eyes skyward.

"Oh, I guess we can start now. Have you given any more thought to your education, Jo Beth?"

"Plenty. I still don't agree with your plan. You and Mom know that I've always wanted to be an actress and I want the education that best prepares me for that career."

She brushed aside a lock of the dirty blond hair that grazed her shoulders and always looked like it could stand a turn with a comb. Her signature navy blue sweat suit, which, at a size too large, draped on her like it would on the hanger, belied a rock hard body trained on dance floors and gym mats at her high school. She didn't stand out in a crowd.

"You never saw Jo Beth coming," said a classmate. "But at the end of the day, she's the only one you remembered."

Roxana had given Jo Beth an early start by reading to her on a daily basis even before pre-school and, consistent with members of her profession, stressed the value of reading. "Books are your friends," she told Jo Beth over and over. "All leaders are readers."

Soon, Jo Beth could read alone and by first grade she had sped right by her classmates and taken a lead she would never relinquish. She checked out several books per week even during the school year. This fed a growing interest in everything around her.

"I can't wait to grow up and explore the world for myself," she repeated.

No topic escaped her interest from the sciences to politics to fine arts. At age twelve she knew more economics and foreign policy than her more famous neighbor out on the farm, which might not be saying much. Even as a teenager she could discuss current events with adult family friends, often times debating them, much to the chagrin of her parents.

The acting thing had started by chance in fourth grade when at the last minute Jo Beth substituted for a friend in a school play. With little preparation she performed her role without a hitch. After that, she entered every play she could, taking roles like Juliette, Lady Macbeth and Cleopatra. Soon, acting had become her passion. Her depth and breadth in different parts got the attention of the drama department at Baylor University in nearby Waco where, while in high school, she participated in summer plays.

The curiosity and adventurous spirit nearly landed her and some friends in the county slammer, an incident that weighed heavily in her parents' choice of colleges. Jo Beth and several band members who had played at a high school party decided to experiment with the selectively bred yield of her garden, which had evaded her parents' detection. Some erratic driving drew the attention of the McLennan County sheriff who was about to detain the group for induction into the criminal justice system when he recognized Jo Beth. He and Billy Bob hunted together.

"Anybody but Sheriff Buford," said Billy Bob, "and you and your friends got a drug record that follows you everywhere."

But the marijuana thing didn't bother the parents nearly as much as her choice of boyfriends. Her current squeeze specialized in the electric guitar and spiked, purple hair. Billy Bob, long time critic of his daughter's taste in music—and boys—took a double shot.

"That crap you and your friends call music oughtta be banned. Whatever happened to Patsy Cline and Ronnie Millsap? Faith Hill not good enough for you?

"And that boyfriend with that hair and prancin' around on stage half nekkid—if he wants to look like a woman why don't he get one of them . . . operations? You girls love that filth 'cause you watch too many of them rock videos."

Consequently, Billy Bob preferred his daughter on a hundred-mile leash in Austin rather than a thirteen hundred mile leash in New York City for the extent of her college days.

"You know our policy on this. We told you before you applied to that school in New York that if you wanted to go there, you're on your own. What changed your mind since our last talk, Jo Beth? Your mother and I had convinced you to find a real major and go to school in a city where family values mean something."

"You silenced me, father, you didn't convince me."

"It's time to get serious, Jo Beth," Roxana said. "You'll be the first in our family to attend college. A young lady in Crawford can hope for nothing greater than a four-year degree in education at the university, then come back here and teach li'l school children. You're far too smart, Jo Beth. Don't waste your brains on actin'."

"Tell that to Sigourney Weaver or Mira Sorvino. But I guess they wasted their brains."

"Who the heck are they?" asked Billy Bob.

"Never mind," Jo Beth said.

"What kind of football team did this Juilliard school have last year?"

"They don't play football there, father. Juilliard is a performing arts school—music, drama, dance, opera . . . "

"What self respectin' school don't have a football team?"

Billy Bob, like all Longhorn fans, looked forward to every September, but more than ever this year. After a middling record the year before earned them a trip to the

CarQuest Bowl where they lost to Fresno State, the alumni and boosters turned up the heat.

"The Texas Longhorns don't play in 'Finger Bowls' or 'Toilet Bowls,'" said one alumni spokesman. "They play in BCS championship games . . . and win!"

The message included a suggestion that the Longhorns open up the offense after decades of boring, three-yards-and-a-cloud-of-dust football and the wins would follow as though the two were joined at the hip. If the status quo persisted, however, the powers that be would change the coaching staff.

The true flashpoint occurred when disgruntled UT law students composed an open letter to the coaches and sent it to the school paper, which gleefully published it. The letter stated that the forward pass had in fact been legalized (in 1908), and cited the relevant statute, article and section of the NCAA rules. The archaic language and sarcasm made the letter the talk of campus. Major Texas newspapers picked it up and printed it. After several weeks of "no comment," head coach Bubba Beefcake promised: "Things will be different in Austin this fall."

To back it up, he and his staff conducted winter drills and spring practice like a survival school. Then they put the heavy acid on the top high school prospects and hit the lottery when Isaiah Jackson, blue chip quarterback from a high school in inner city Houston, picked Texas over a hundred other schools who bid for his services. He had rewritten all Texas high school passing records and his signing gave notice to other hot recruits in the

Southwest that things would indeed be different in Austin that year and they followed him.

"We chased the slackers and hangers-on and now we got nothing but winners," said Beefcake. The off season changes brought Longhorn football all the way into the new century when most supporters would have given a standing ovation if it had just come into the last century.

"Jo Beth, your pappy can already picture hisself at Memorial Stadium on Saturdays for the next four years yellin' 'Hook 'em Horns.' Don't take that from me!"

"This isn't about you, father."

"How can you ever leave this beautiful, historic town for that toilet, that cesspool, that . . . that Sodom and Gomorrah? You know, Jo Beth, we had a President from right here in Crawford."

"Don't remind me. And his move from Washington back to Crawford raised the IQ of both places."

"See, I told you he was smart," said Billy Bob. Jo Beth just smiled.

"When members at First Baptist find out that my daughter's goin' to New York, they'll pick a new deacon."

"Yes, darling," said Roxana. "What about your family? What will the neighbors think? If you run off to that place it could hurt our standin' in the community."

"I've read so much about other places I can't wait to see them. New York and California really interest me; so much diversity. Besides, I want to live in a blue state."

"California!" said Billy Bob. "All that's out there is commies and queers!"

"Jo Beth," said Roxana, "all you need to know about New York is in Revelations 18: 'Babylon the great is fallen, is fallen and is become the habitation of devils and every foul spirit and the cage of every unclean and hateful bird.' "

"You know, for all the bad things you attribute to New York, there still must be ten thousand churches in that city, so it can't be all bad. Why don't you give it a chance?"

"Crawford's good enough for us, and if it's good enough for us, it's good enough for you. If you go to New York, I don't show my face at our meetins." Billy Bob took a long hit of Pearl.

"You don't show it now, father. You always wear that white sheet. Besides, those rednecks you call friends would sell you out in a heartbeat, grand dragon or not. You saw how they treated you after my speech!"

Billy Bob sprayed the area with that long hit of Pearl. "Rednecks! You've crossed a line with that one, young lady. Those are God-fearin' Christians who love their country."

"Yes, father, they love America but they hate most of the people in it."

Longhorn fan Billy Bob Lester did his own version of three-yards-and-a-cloud-of-dust. "Forgive her, Lord," he incanted. "My daughter's a blasphemer. Talk like that can get us run out of town."

"Like we told you," Roxana said, "we'd support this actin' thing until graduation, but then you had to consider the responsibilities of a young lady."

"Jo Beth, you go to New York and you get no help from us," Billy Bob said, and drained the can of Pearl.

As the discussion progressed, Jo Beth's expression dropped from enthusiasm to dejection to depression. Tears ran down her cheeks as her parents heaped one more piece of bad news on top of another.

"Yes, darlin', I agree with your daddy. You have the rest of the summer to change your mind. If you do as we suggest, we'll forgive you and help you all we can. If you want to do things your way, you're on your own."

Jo Beth went silent. She walked to her bedroom and seemed not to come out for several days and moped about the house well into summer. Her parents knew their daughter and her passion for the stage well enough to understand that their decision could leave a scar.

"Billy Bob, you know that for all of her wonderful qualities, Jo Beth doesn't forgive. She still holds grudges against friends going back to childhood. Do you think she'll believe that we're being unfair?"

"She'll come around, Roxana. Once she thinks about it, she'll realize that she can get just as much in Austin as she can in New York. We can take comfort in our decision."

A month later, Jo Beth came to her parents. "I've changed my mind. I'll go to Austin and major in education."

"We knew you'd see things our way, darling. You've just made Billy Bob and me the proudest, happiest parents in the state of Texas."

After a hot summer in Crawford, Billy Bob and Roxana drove their daughter and her belongings one hundred miles south to the campus in Austin. For a week she fought through the bureaucracy of registration and the logistics of relocation. When it was all over she reached into her folder of paper work, fished out her athletic events card, and slipped it to Billy Bob.

"I'll never use this thing. You'll be right in the middle of screaming freshmen for at least the first year, father. I'll try to do better next year."

"Don't make no nevermind to me. I'll just be happy to be here."

The gesture not only got Billy Bob next to his beloved Longhorns but to him it signaled that his daughter had sublimated any hostilities she might have harbored with her parents' management of her life.

The years that followed saw Billy Bob in better and better accommodations at Memorial Stadium. Jo Beth expanded her network to include more of the athletic department and her sophomore year she scored seats in the south end zone about fifteen rows up. Texas students joked that from there you couldn't see the field for the curvature of the earth, but it still didn't make no nevermind to Billy Bob. He parceled out extras to friends and colleagues, thus raising his stock in the community. Nothing speaks currency in Texas like Longhorn football tickets. While Jo Beth was the honor student in Austin, Billy Bob was The Man in Crawford.

Isaiah Jackson, meanwhile, fulfilled all the prophecies. He and his classmates brought the Longhorns conference championships and a return to BCS bowl games for the next four years. Yes, he stayed all four years in spite of lures from NFL scouts and agents. From the day he arrived in Austin, everyone wanted a piece of him and encouraged him to jump early but Isaiah held them off. He made it clear from the start that he would graduate from Texas on schedule, because the degree meant insurance against a debilitating injury and it would set an example for youngsters. He would think about the NFL in four years. The coaches celebrated his decision. A grateful Billy Bob Lester said, "Ain't he the greatest!"

On football weekends Roxana made the drive to Austin with Billy Bob and while he did his Longhorn thing with the good ol' boys, she spent afternoons with Jo Beth shopping and getting the dime tour of the area.

In four years Billy Bob and Roxana never had to endure those torments that keep parents awake at night. No calls from the Dean of Students, the police department or the county coroner. In fact, only straight "A" grade reports followed by a certificate that read, "Dean's List of Scholars," provided the only correspondence from the university to Billy Bob and Roxana.

When graduation week arrived, the parents drove to Austin for the event they had anticipated for the last four years: Jo Beth receiving her diploma with honors. They would spend the week in Austin, attend commencement and maybe some graduation parties, then gather their daughter's estate, along with their daughter, and haul everything back to Crawford where Jo Beth would begin her teaching career. Once again the nest would be full.

The first clue that their weekend travel package might not include Paradise dropped when Jo Beth told Billy Bob and Roxana that she had a boyfriend. "He graduates this week and then he starts a great job."

"You never told us about a boyfriend," said Roxana. Mom should have taken clues from Jo Beth's high school days when her daughter rarely suffered from male neglect.

"It must have slipped my mind. I've been so busy and all. We've been dating for about two years. We'll be having dinner with him and his family after the ceremony on Sunday. You'll like him, father."

"Just so it ain't one of them rock stars," said Billy Bob. Jo Beth smiled.

On graduation day the proud parents accompanied their daughter to the building where the ceremony would take place. At least four hundred people milled about the theater.

"Why would they hold your graduation in the theater, darlin'?" said Roxana. "Your department is Education."

"I had a double major, Education *and* Theater! I've chosen to accept my degree at the Theater Arts ceremony. You know I've always wanted to be an actress."

Billy Bob and Roxana couldn't believe their ears.

"Let's meet here right after the ceremony. You'll get to meet my boyfriend and his family."

The stunned couple half-heartedly agreed to Jo Beth's plan as they seemed unable to assimilate the last piece of news. They sat in the audience for the duration and when the speaker announced, "Jo Beth Lester, B. A., Theater Arts and Education, Summa Cum Laude," they let out a muted cheer while the rest of the audience lifted the roof.

Afterwards they met a beaming Jo Beth at the assigned place and the three awaited her boyfriend and his family. An uneasy silence hung over them as other buildings around the quad emptied their congregations. The area turned into a beehive.

As Billy Bob surveyed the landscape he became animated and grabbed Jo Beth's arm. "Hey, Jo Beth, ain't that Isaiah Jackson over there?"

Jo Beth looked in that direction. "That's him, the one, the only!"

The familiar All American quarterback, all 6' 6" of him in his cap and gown, stood tall like the Texas Tower amid family, friends, and jock sniffers, about a first-down away from the Lesters.

"I know he's tied up but do you think you could get me his autograph? I'd be honored."

"I don't think he'd mind. He was in some of my classes."

Jo Beth strode over to Isaiah's group and cut right through, as though she had a press pass made of gold. She whispered something to Isaiah and led him in the direction of Billy Bob and Roxana. Billy Bob almost wet himself. When they arrived, Jo Beth began the introductions.

"Mom, dad, I'd like you to meet my boyfriend, Isaiah Jackson. Isaiah, this is my mom and dad, Roxana and Billy Bob Lester. Ike, my father thinks you're the greatest thing ever to hit Texas football. Father, you might want to thank Isaiah for those great seats you've had at Memorial Stadium."

Billy Bob *did* wet himself. He and Roxana looked like they had just stuck their fingers in a light socket. Their jaws dropped, their eyes flew open, their hair frizzed out and they stood paralyzed as their lives unraveled before them. Robotically, Billy Bob shook hands with Isaiah as did Roxana. When Isaiah's group arrived seconds later, he introduced his family to the Lesters. Discomfort reigned as the Lesters and the Jacksons carried out their own rendition of *Guess Who's Coming to Dinner.*

Reporters from newspapers throughout Texas showed up to record the moment when hometown graduates collected their diplomas and other honors. Flashbulbs popped all over the quadrangle. Doting parents couldn't get enough shots of their kids in cap and gown. Billy Bob's new digital camera, which he bought just for the occasion, seemed to have malfunctioned, so Jo Beth jumped into the breach. She yelled at a reporter with whom she had worked as a high school intern at the Crawford Demagogue. He came over and snapped several pictures of Jo Beth, Isaiah, and the families. Neither Billy Bob nor Roxana ducked fast enough.

The families dined that evening at the Texas Land and Cattle Company, the premier steak house in Austin, and silence reigned. People at adjacent tables kept pointing at Isaiah and coming to him for autographs.

At a lull in the activity, Billy Bob got his daughter's attention. "Jo Beth, we're going to be heading back to Crawford right after dinner. Are you packed and ready?"

"Uh . . . not exactly, father. I won't be going back to Crawford."

Another bombshell for the folks. "Then you'll be joining us in a few days? You have to sign up and fill out papers so you can start teachin' in September."

"I won't be teaching. Ike and I are flying to New York on Wednesday." Jo Beth snuggled next to her man. "He starts his first mini camp with the Jets. They made him their first overall pick in this year's NFL draft. At the same time, I'll be starting my career on the stages of the Big Apple."

That was about ten bombshells too many for the parents. After that piece of news, the evening and the trip to Austin couldn't end soon enough for Roxana and Billy Bob. The parents said their goodbyes and beat feet back to Crawford that night to plot damage control. Wait a minute! Hadn't their daughter just graduated summa cum laude from a major university, hooked up with a multi millionaire, and planned to take off with him to New York City, each to start a career in jobs that they loved, miles ahead of the competition?

Billy Bob and Roxana awakened early the next morning and grabbed their copy of the newspaper the second it hit the porch. They opened it and there, on the front page of the sports section, Isaiah Jackson in his cap and gown with his arm around, as the caption read, "Crawford's own Jo Beth Lester, Theater Arts graduate and summa cum laude," as Billy Bob and Roxana looked on.

"Everybody's gonna see this, Roxana. What can we do?"

"Well, we still got an hour before dawn. Let's go door to door to door and steal all the newspapers we can until the sun comes up."

"Good idea. Then let's pray that no one else in Crawford reads the paper today." Those prayers were not answered.

Billy Bob got a cool reception at work from just about everyone. Although none of his colleagues broached the topic with him directly, he knew they were talking about it behind his back. Roxana got a similar response at her school, at her exercise class, and at her weekly meeting of the Flat Earth Society. Everybody knew everybody in Crawford.

Roxana and Billy Bob went to bed that night trying to sort out the events of the last several days, each trying to assuage an uncertain conscience. They talked about Jo Beth's long running deception, her choice of boyfriend, and her move to New York, but never called into question their own policies.

"When she comes back after her failed attempt in the big city," said Roxana, "we will forgive her because we are Christians and that's what Christians do."

"And we will welcome her back into the fold," said Billy Bob.

"If nothing else, Billy Bob, we can take some pride in having raised a self reliant and independent, if headstrong, daughter, and maybe we should think twice about attending any more of her graduations."

They drifted off to sleep some time around midnight, unaware that yet another bombshell hovered at low altitude. At about 2:00 a.m. they were awakened by a ruckus in their front yard. They could see a bright light coming from that direction. Billy Bob shot out of bed and stumbled toward the window where he witnessed, on his very own lawn—that of the grand dragon—a cross, blazing away, just like the many he'd help set on other lawns. So brightly did it burn that he could barely make out three figures in white sheets walking away from the scene accompanied by the fading strains of a harmonica blowing "Dixie," something he'd heard dozens of times, only at those times he had walked next to the musician.

Then he remembered Jo Beth's prediction about those rednecks.

Lynne Grant-Westenhaver

Lynne Grant-Westenhaver's background as an author began in high school, where she wrote a weekly column for a local newspaper.

She studied journalism at San Jose State, and has written for many venues over the years. Most recently, Lynne has focused on fiction. Short stories, novelettes and flash fiction are her favorite genres.

She was born in San Francisco and now resides in Pleasant Hill, California; but considers Hawaii, where her family lives, her real home.

Saving Charlie

❧

It was the summer of 1941. Charlie had just turned twelve. His best pal—the one person who had always stood up for him—his brother, Joey, had enlisted in the Navy that day. Charlie was proud of Joey's decision, but his parents were adamantly against it. Mom wept. Furious with Joey, Pop pounded his fist heavily on the kitchen table and shouted, "No!"

But Joey had a mind of his own and he loved his country.

"I report tomorrow, Pop," Joey said. "I want you and Mom to be there to see me off, but if you decide your anger is going to get in the way, then I'll go to the train station alone."

"I'll be there, Joey. You can count on me." Charlie threw his arms around his brother's waist.

"Hey squirt! I know I can." His mom cried even harder. "Mom, please don't take this so hard. I'll be back; I promise."

"You're only nineteen, Joey."

"I'm not the only nineteen year old guy going, Mom."

"Mom . . . " Charlie started to speak.

"Charlie, don't bother me. Go to your room," Mom said, biting her lip and twisting the end of her apron.

"But, Mom, I want to stay with Joey."

"I said go to your room." Charlie dropped his head and slowly walked out of the kitchen.

"Listen, son." Pop spoke slowly, his anger subsiding. "You know my feelings. I can't stop you. You're of age." He took a deep breath and put his hand on Joey's shoulder. "I pray that you return safe, son; you can see your mom is taking it very hard. Sit with her a while." With that, Joey's father stood and walked out of the room, slamming the door as he left.

⊶ ⊶ ⊶

Charlie spent a restless night. It would be hard not having Joey there. Joey took care of him. He made sure that Pop didn't get too carried away taking out his temper on Charlie. Pop would always apologize after his outbursts, but Joey was afraid that one of these days Pop would haul off and hit Charlie so hard he wouldn't be able to take it back. It worried him. He didn't want to leave without having some guarantee this wouldn't happen. Mom felt helpless when it came to Pop's temper. He would never hit her but he had no qualms about hitting Charlie. How many times had Joey grabbed Pop and held him back?

Joey hadn't told Charlie or Pop that arrangements had been made to send Charlie off to Mom's cousins on Long Island. They were good Christian people who would take care of Charlie. Uncle Ed was a pastor. When Mom called and explained about Charlie and Pop, the

Whitfield's were happy to rescue him from this potentially dangerous situation. They knew Pop was a good man but they also knew he had a violent temper which, more often than not, got the best of him, and Charlie always seemed to be the receiver of his heated outbursts.

When Pop got into a rage, Mom would holler at him, but he always ignored her. Once she tried to stop Pop from hitting Charlie and ended up with a black eye. Pop had not meant to hit her. He spent the entire evening on his knees that night begging her for forgiveness. Charlie wasn't so fortunate. The doctor said that his ribs were not broken, but could have been. On his way out, the doctor confronted Pop telling him if this ever happened again he would find himself behind bars.

Early the morning of Joey's departure, he knocked on Charlie's door and quietly let himself in.

"Charlie, you awake?" Charlie moaned and turned over to face him.

"Hi Joey," Charlie said, rubbing the sleep from his eyes.

"Listen, Squirt. I have something to tell you and I want you to take it like the Boy Scout that I know you are."

Charlie sat up. "What is it, Joey?"

"You're going away for a while. I made arrangements with Mom to contact our cousins on Long Island. You know the Whitfields."

"Yeah, Mom talks about them but I don't remember ever meeting them."

"You only met them once when you were real young."

"Well," Joey took a long breath, "you're going to be staying with them for a while, Squirt, and they are happy that you're coming. Uncle Ed told me they look forward to it."

"Why am I going, Joey?"

"Because I don't want Pop to lose his temper and take it out on you. I won't be here and I don't want anything to happen to you."

Charlie thought about what Joey had just said. Tears welled in his eyes. He tried to hold them back.

"Joey. I'm going to miss you but I'll make you proud of me, I promise. I'll show you I'm a good Boy Scout. You can depend on me."

"You won't let me down Squirt. I know that."

The brothers hugged each other, their cheeks wet with tears.

❦ ❦ ❦

The train station was packed. So many young men shipping out. Some for basic training others to unknown destinations in Europe and the South Pacific. Charlie was caught up in the pandemonium of it. He held tight to Joey's hand.

"I'm gonna miss you, Charlie." Joey looked down at him.

"Will you write me a letter sometime, Joey?"

"You bet. I'll write you every week and I'll airmail it to the Whitfield's in New York." Charlie grinned.

"That'd be great, Joey."

Joey stopped and turned toward his parents who followed closely behind.

"Well folks, I guess I'd better say good bye; everyone is starting to board." Joey gave Mom a hug. She had started crying.

"Mom, I'll see you again right before I'm sent overseas, so don't think you're rid of me yet." She managed a smile and tucked a little bag of homemade cookies in his hand.

"Your favorite kind, Joey." He kissed her. "Thanks, Mom."

"Pop." Joey held out his hand. His father stood stiff and unrelenting.

"Well, I said my piece, son. You know I'll miss you but I've said all I'm saying." He shook Joey's hand and turned to leave. Mom stayed with Charlie, their eyes locked on Joey as they watched him board the train. Soldiers and sailors were hanging out windows throwing kisses and waves to loved ones. Charlie looked for Joey but he had melted into the crowd. The heroic scene made an indelible impression on him. *If only I was old enough to go too,* he thought.

☛ ☛ ☛

Pastor Ed Whitfield and his wife Louise were known throughout their community of Sandy Beach, as people the Lord had blessed. And that blessing rested on everyone that fell under Ed Whitfield's pastorship. Indeed he was sought out by his parishioners and known to be a kind and generous man.

When Ed announced to his daughters that their cousin, Charlie, his sister's son from Rochester, would be coming to live with them they were skeptical. Janie, the youngest, was the only one who didn't ask why. Even though she didn't remember Charlie, she was delighted at the prospect of her cousin's arrival. She couldn't wait until her family picked him up at Grand Central Station the next day.

"Do you think Charlie remembers us, Dad?"

"Charlie was about two or three when my sister and her family were here last. So he probably doesn't."

"Good," Janie exclaimed. "We can start out fresh."

●◇ ●◇ ●◇

Charlie could hardly sleep the night before he left so he rose from bed early. Two neatly packed suitcases stood ready by the door. Mom told him he could take the special Boy Scout pack with the scout emblem sewn on it that she had made for him when he joined the Rochester troop. He was happy to take it. That and his baseball mitt were the only possessions he owned that mattered.

He hoped he would be able to join a scout troop in Sandy Beach. Pop made him leave the troop in Rochester. He said it was a waste of time. Charlie loved his troop and it broke his heart to have to give it up. Pop had been extra mean to him the last few days. But he had only smacked him once. Charlie was relieved by that. He would miss Mom but he could hardly wait to get away from Pop. He prayed that Uncle Ed would be nicer to him and trusted what Joey said about Uncle Ed being a nice man. A pastor. He didn't know much about pastors.

He quickly stuffed the few Superman comic books he had into the backpack along with his baseball mitt and the small bag of gumdrops Mom had given him. His favorite. He carefully placed them along side the comic books, took one last look at his room and closed the door.

●◇ ●◇ ●◇

The train ride to New York City was long and boring. The only good part was the gumdrops. He reached into the backpack to make sure they were still there. He decided the only way to get through the trip was to bury himself in the adventures of Superman and eat the gumdrops slowly one at a time.

He must have dozed off because the next sound he heard was the porter calling out Grand Central. He elongated each syllable. *Judging from his looks he must have been calling out the station for centuries,* Charlie thought. He stopped at Charlie's seat.

"You Charles?"

"Yes Sir."

"I'm in charge of getting you to the party that's meeting you under the big clock young man. So be ready to get off when the train stops."

Charlie nodded. He could have handled meeting up with his cousins himself. He wasn't some kid. Besides, he wanted to take a look at the dome inside the station. Joey had told him to be sure to see it.

The train began slowing down. Charlie could feel the jerky motion of the brakes under his feet then the long whistle caused by the steam escaping from the engine. Suddenly the train came to an abrupt halt. The porter helped him with his suitcases and guided him down the steps onto the platform. Charlie looked up and there before him were more people then he ever knew existed. Men in suits; ladies dressed up wearing hats looking like they were going to meet the President or something. He couldn't take his eyes off their red lips and pink cheeks. The men were wearing hats too. Some carried small cases. It was almost like Sunday morning at church, he thought, except the farm folks that attended the church in Rochester weren't dressed as nice. Everyone seemed to be smoking. There was smoke everywhere he turned. He couldn't get away from it.

People were rushing toward the train. The ones that had gotten off were rushing toward the station, *Just like him and the porter. Wow, what a mess.* The porter held Charlie's arm to keep them from being separated. Men and women in uniform stood in small groups inside the station. Charlie wondered if they were waiting to be shipped out. It reminded him of Joey boarding the train. Tears began to fill his eyes and he quickly ran his sleeve over his face and said a little prayer for Joey. He missed him.

It took a lot of effort to reach the big clock. It was hard pushing through the crowds. Charlie almost lost his scout pack when some guy in a hurry knocked against him and kicked the pack across the floor. The porter rushed after it and almost lost sight of Charlie but in the end they arrived at the big clock. The porter pulled out a sign from his pocket which had "Whitfield" stamped on it. He held it high in the air above the heads of the travelers so Charlie's cousins could see it.

Standing there, Charlie tilted his head up toward the dome, which seemed to be thousands of feet above him. Joey told him to be sure and look up at the dome. He could not take his eyes off of it. He had never seen anything so beautiful. The constellations and stars painted on it seemed to sparkle even in broad daylight.

Gazing upward with his mouth open, he heard a giggle. His faced turned red. He must have looked like a dummy. Uncle Ed, dressed in a nice suit, smiled at him. Aunt Louise reached out and gave him a hug.

"Charlie, we are so happy you've come to live with us."

Charlie tried to smile but it was hard. He hugged the Boy Scout pack closer to him. He needed to feel something that was familiar. His three cousins stared at him, each with a different expression. Anna was sixteen and pretty with long dark hair and big eyes. Her voice was soft. He kind of liked it. Next was Jessie, fourteen, who blinked her eyes at him and said, "Hi." Last was Janie. She was nine and shorter by a foot than Charlie. A big grin covered her face as she greeted him. She was cute with curly blond hair and he liked her at once.

"I am so happy you're here," she said excitedly. "I want to show you where the cave is when we get home." Then she leaned close to him and whispered, "It's hidden and secret."

"Janie, what have I told you. You are not to talk about that cave," Uncle Ed sharply reprimanded her. "Didn't you promise me?"

"I just want to show Charlie where it is on top of the mountain, Dad." Looking at Charlie, she finished with, "We're not suppose to go there because it is very dangerous."

Uncle Ed thanked the porter, gave him a tip, and escorted everyone out of the terminal.

●◇ ●◇ ●◇

Sandy Beach was a small town that sat along the eastern seaboard. The town boasted three thousand inhabitants. Two thousand of those were permanents or "year rounders." Summer dwellers accounted for the rest. His cousins' pretty white two-story house was set far back from the street to provide privacy. Tall trees fronted the circular driveway and colorful flowers edged the stone walkway leading to the front door. Charlie liked the way it looked. It sat on a tree-lined street next to a beach access road.

"Come along, Charlie." Uncle Ed picked up the suitcases and started toward the house. Janie ran ahead.

"Can I show him, Dad? Can I show him his room?"

"All right then, hurry up. You can open the front door."

Charlie was greeted by two barking dogs sniffing and jumping up on him.

"That's Toad and Randolph. They won't hurt you." Janie pulled each dog away and pushed them out the door.

"Come on!" Janie urged. "Your room is at the top of the stairs. It used to be the guest bedroom but now it's yours. We hope you like it." Uncle Ed followed with the bags and set them down on the bed.

"Can I help you unpack, Charlie, can I?"

"Janie, if Charlie doesn't mind we will both help him." Aunt Louise stood by the door smiling. "We hope you're going to enjoy being with us, Charlie."

He didn't know what to say. He had never had such a nice room. It was kind of like a boy's room should be. There were even posters on the wall of cars and things.

"We decorated the way we thought you might like it, but if you don't we can change it."

"Oh no, ma'am. I really like it. Thank you."

●❖ ●❖ ●❖

The days that followed were the best that Charlie had ever known. The awkwardness that had overwhelmed him at first soon disappeared. He was starting to relax. This was a feeling he had not experienced because he was always on edge around Pop, never knowing when Pop's hand would come down hard. No matter what Charlie did or said, it was always the wrong thing. Now he was with a family that cared about him. He even got a special introduction at Uncle Ed's church and all the people had applauded. To his delight, Charlie discovered that Uncle Ed was also the leader of the church's scout troop of eight boys. Each of them carried a pair of binoculars. When Charlie asked about it, Uncle Ed handed him a pair and explained they were to be used for spotting enemy submarines. Scouts that lived in coastal cities had been requested to help the coast guard. It was their civic duty for the war effort. Charlie was all for that. He was determined to be a good spotter so Joey would be proud of him.

Uncle Ed had planned a special campout on the beach to welcome him to the troop several weeks after his arrival.

"I thought you and the other boys would enjoy it," Uncle Ed had said. Charlie could hardly wait. Sitting around the campfire with the other boys singing songs and telling stories instilled an instant camaraderie. He realized that these scouts were becoming real friends. He had never had friends before. And he wanted to do his best not only for his new friends but also for Joey and

Uncle Ed. Uncle Ed was easy to talk to. Charlie could ask questions without the fear of being called stupid.

The soft sound of waves gently touching the shore began to lull him to sleep. A slight breeze took away the heat the day had left behind. The background whispers and laughter that permeated the campsite were welcome intrusions as the boys began to settle down for the night, but Charlie's sleep was suddenly interrupted when he heard nearby voices discussing the cave. He opened his eyes and sat up, ready to ask questions about the cave's location, but just then Uncle Ed came by and silenced them.

●◇ ●◇ ●◇

Charlie was like a big brother to Janie. She looked up to him. He had become her best friend. Her sisters remained busy with their friends and considered Janie and Charlie children, which was fine with them. They walked daily from one end of the beach to the other looking for shells, or running head on into the waves that washed over them leaving the taste of salty sand in their mouths. Charlie loved swimming out beyond the breakers but Janie wouldn't follow. She'd stand on the beach and make crazy faces at him.

Each week a letter from Joey arrived just like Joey said it would. Janie listened while Charlie read it out loud. Then he'd go to his room and write back. He told Joey about becoming a spotter and how he planned on finding a good place to track enemy submarines. One afternoon

270

with this thought in mind and how he could make Joey proud, he approached Janie. She was standing near the path that led to the beach.

"When are we going to the cave, Janie?" She looked wide-eyed, almost surprised that he'd asked.

"I thought you wanted to show me where it is?" She hesitated.

"I do, Charlie, but Dad said no. It's too dangerous."

"Why is it dangerous?" She started to walk toward the beach. Charlie followed her. Finally she stopped and turned to him.

"A boy was killed there."

"How?"

"He tried to reach the cave from the ocean side. There are two entrances: one from a steep climb up the mountain and the other a very narrow path that overhangs the ocean. It's about a fifty-foot drop. There are lots of jagged rocks that jut into the ocean. The boy's friends dared him to take the ocean path, which is only about a foot wide. It curves around the side of the mountain, which has a sheer rock face. There is nothing to hold onto. It's like walking a tightrope."

Charlie thought about the scene Janie had just described.

"But I could climb up using the mountain path . . . right?"

"Well, I don't know." She thought about it for a minute, then shook her head no.

"My Father wouldn't like it."

"I could do it, if you showed me where to go. We'll tell your folks that I'm going camping."

"But what if you get hurt, Charlie? I would be in so much trouble and so would you."

"I'm not going to get hurt. The cave will be a good place to look for enemy submarines and I will be doing my civic duty as a Boy Scout. Uncle Ed asked us to use the binoculars for this exact thing. I had survival training and climbing experience with the troop in Rochester. I'm practically a professional outdoorsman," Charlie boasted. "You can trust me, Janie."

That Saturday morning Charlie and Janie got up before sunrise.

"We're going to take the beach path. Then take the cutoff that veers toward the woods."

"Why are we going through the woods?" Charlie asked.

"Because that's the way that leads to the mountain trail. You'll see Charlie, just follow me."

It had rained the night before and the ground was damp. The path was covered with leaves and smelled of decaying mulch and pine. The sun was beginning to peek through the canopy of branches that covered the forest and they could hear small animals scurrying about foraging for food. As they continued along the trail, the branches began to open up allowing the sun to take over. Then all of a sudden they stood in a clearing that footed the tallest mountain Charlie had ever seen. He couldn't take his eyes off of it.

Climbing it would be a major challenge. Its rocky ledges allowed hikers to manage the climb—that was the good part. The bad part was there didn't seem to be a carved out trail. It would take all day to climb, in any case.

"Where's the cave?" Charlie couldn't see any openings on the top from where he stood.

"All I know is that it is on the other side of the trail just past the fork. You have to stay straight and keep to your left."

As they walked back, Janie kept looking at Charlie. The thought of Charlie on that mountain horrified her. What would her father say if he found out? That thought horrified her even more.

"Janie, will you monitor me? I'll write down the climbing route as best I can so you can keep track. Meet me here late afternoon tomorrow. If I'm not down by then, tell your father."

"If you get hurt I will never forgive myself. Not to mention what Father will do."

The next morning, Janie and Charlie started out just as the sun was dividing lacey shadows over the forest floor into streams of light. The smell of pine needles wafted gently through the morning air. It seemed to take only minutes before they came to the end of the forest trail emerging into the bright sunlight of the open field.

"Are you going to be okay monitoring me, Janie? I know you're not happy about my going up there but I promise I'll be real careful. Sighting an enemy sub will sure make Joey and Uncle Ed proud of me. I should be back down by early afternoon. Tell Aunt Louise thanks for the blanket, food and water. Tell her I found a good place to camp. Remember Janie, start back before it gets late. I don't want you to get in trouble."

"Charlie, I'm only helping you because I trust you. Please be careful." With that said, Janie helped Charlie on with the pack.

"Well Janie, I guess I'm set. Don't worry."

Despite his confidence, he somehow felt as if he was saying his last goodbye. That didn't make sense, so he shrugged it off.

"I'll see you tomorrow." Janie's words echoed behind following him onto the trail.

◆◆ ◆◆ ◆◆

The trail going up was not what it had seemed. It was eighty percent more difficult and extremely steep in places that were not visible from the ground. He hadn't calculated this into his arrival time. On one of the turns he almost slipped. Grabbing the branch of one of the taller trees that grew far below he was able to steady himself. The level parts of the trail gave him a chance to make up time, but there were few of them, and even then, he had to hold tight to bushes and small plants that grew along the ridge to keep from tumbling down the mountainside.

The face of the mountain was rocky. The trail, a narrow dirt path, was forged by other hikers who Charlie knew were much braver and more experienced then he. An eerie feeling of total exposure overcame him. He couldn't deny it. The trail was steep and he was scared. The higher he climbed the more frightened he became. He kept looking up to see if he could determine where the opening of the cave was. The sun was beginning to veer off to the west which meant it was getting late and he had a long way yet to go. He had to make it to the top before sunset. What if he couldn't make it before dark?

That thought made his stomach wrench. There was no way he could climb at night; the trail was too unpredictable and there was no clear-cut path. So far it had not offered a place that was flat enough to spread out. He had to keep moving, only stopping a couple of times to take water. He was getting hungry and the pack was becoming heavier. He looked down. The drop was significant—so much so that the trees looked like miniature pieces on a game board that could be moved around at the slightest touch. Goosebumps covered his skin. Frightened, Charlie knew he had to keep moving. The trail had become so steep he had to lie flat against the ground and crawl up the last part. The sun was setting, filling random clouds with extraordinary colors or oranges, purples, pinks. The beauty of the colors gave him hope.

"Wow." The sound of his voice echoed. "What a view. What a sunset." His voice reverberated back reeling off the mountain into space. Charlie had never seen anything so magnificent. *This must be the way God sees it,* he thought. *Am I that high up? I must be.*

And then he saw it. The cave opening was right in front of him. He looked inside. It was mostly dark but he could see the sunset from the opening on the ocean side. Inching in slowly on his hands and knees, he looked around, even checking above to make sure it was safe. Everything seemed secure. The floor of the cave was flat and covered in dirt. It was a small space, but there was room enough to spread out. He worked his way in to the ocean side and gasped.

There before him lay a panoramic view of the Atlantic bathed in shimmering moonlight, the effervescent glow illuminating its vastness making each ripple sparkle and twinkle just like the night sky above him. The stars seemed so close he felt he could reach out and touch them. He had never seen so many. It reminded him of the dome ceiling at Grand Central Station. He could never have imagined this. He was on top of the world—just him and God.

Charlie hadn't thought about eating. There was no way he could have managed it on the way up but now his stomach screamed at him. Crouching down on his knees, he pulled the pack around so that he could release it over his arms. The space in the cave was not high enough to let him stand but he could kneel. He spread out the tarp that Aunt Louise had packed so he could eat comfortably and still look out at the galaxy of stars. With the last bite gone he lay down on the tarp to admire the vision that stretched out before him. Total quietness surrounded him. A coolness began creeping into the cave. It would be a colder night then he had prepared for. But he was a Boy Scout, after all. He could handle it.

Charlie zipped up his jacket and wrapped the tarp around him. He reasoned with sunrise all the cold would dissipate. He just had to make it through the night and he could do that, he determined in his twelve-year-old mind. He was exhausted. Sleep came easily and he drifted into dreamlessness. It was the thundering sound that startled him. His eyes did not want to open so he pulled the tarp closer trying to slide under it. But the sound became louder. He couldn't grasp what was happening when suddenly what seemed to be hundreds of bats immediately swerved and careened over him. As he pushed the tarp away to look, the menacing bats bombarded him. Hundreds of blinding bat eyes charged toward him, surrounding his body. He screamed, and tried to push them away from his face but they remained relentless in their attack. Their wings cocooned him.

Charlie tried to move, to sit up, but he couldn't see. The bats swarmed around his head and face. He yelled, flailing his arms in every direction trying to keep them away from his eyes. He couldn't get onto his knees to inch himself out of the opening. He lunged forward and, as he did, the ground beneath him gave way. To his horror he was airborne and falling. He couldn't believe it. He was going to crash on the rocks and die. No! He didn't want to die! He tried to prepare himself for what he was about to experience, praying it would be fast. Tears streamed down his face.

God, help me! Please. His last thought was of Joey.

∎◦ ∎◦ ∎◦

A cold sharpness that felt like a knife slashed through him. The intensity of the impact filled his lungs and nostrils, jolting his senses into realizing that he was descending rapidly toward the bottom of the ocean. He regained enough rational thought to kick and pull himself upward; trying not to take in any more water and holding his breath until he thought his lungs would explode. He reached the surface just in time. Gasping, the cold night air filled his lungs and brain bringing him back to sanity.

He was shivering, but he was alive and looking up at the star-studded universe as he treaded water trying to gain sight of where in the ocean he had landed. He couldn't make out any images that looked like land and he needed something to hang onto. He didn't have the strength to keep treading water or to determine which way to swim. Then he saw it floating within a foot of him. The scout pack with the bottle of water still inside which kept it from sinking. He grabbed it. At least it was something to hold onto.

After what seemed like hours, but were probably only minutes, he could feel his legs beginning to tingle. He knew what would happen if he didn't get out of the water. He tried again to look for land but was hampered by the waves, which were just high enough to impair his vision.

He didn't have enough strength to swim and, even if he had, it was not the solution. He was pretty sure the current would carry him out even further. But there was nothing he could do. He was scared but not as scared as he had been before hitting the water. *God, you saved me from landing on the rocks. Please don't let me drown. Give me the courage and strength to make it.* As he said this prayer, something nudged his back. He froze. *Please God don't let it be a shark!* The nudge came again. He turned to find a large piece of floating something. It looked like a log. He grabbed hold and tried to pull himself up on top. It took about ten times because it rolled with each wave, but in the end, he was able to straddle it.

He thanked God and held on tight. The next few hours were a blur. He thought he dozed off but even in that dazed state he held onto the log with all of his strength.

❧ ❧ ❧

Shades of light drizzled across the sky. The blanket of stars had disappeared. Images and shapes were becoming discernable. Charlie's eyes stung from salt water. Even afloat on the log, the waves had showered him with salty spray again and again. It didn't matter; he was alive and floating on top of the water, not in it, dealing with hypothermia. Seeing clearly was not easy. The salt smudged his vision but he was beginning to see landmarks. Had he been that close to land?

As he scanned the shoreline more closely he could see what looked like a small beach, possibly a cove. The distance was about the length of a football field from where he was floating. Jagged outcroppings of rocks protected the cove. He should be able to swim there. He lifted his head. The water lay flat, motionless. The waves remained silent in the early morning tide. He thought he could make it to shore easily. His heart pounded. He slid off the log into the cold water.

As soon as his feet touched the sandy beach, he fell down into its softness and slept. When he awoke the sun was directly overhead. He must have slept for several hours. He sat up. His clothes had dried. Charlie sat on the beach for a long while thinking about what to do. The sun had not changed its overhead position and that seemed strange. He was a little tired and needed time to check the rocky ledge that protected the cove. Squinting, he looked up searching the backdrop of jagged crevices. Each one dead-ended midway up to the top. There were no footholds that he could see. The formidable surface of granite, which had carved out and left its signature on these uneven formations centuries ago, had not allowed for easy access, or as far as Charlie could tell, a way to leave without getting back into the ocean.

Struggling with his lack of options, he became determined to find a way out of the cove. Maybe he could wait for the tide to go out then walk along the shoreline until he found a safe place. He wanted desperately to reach home before everyone started worrying. He didn't know how he would explain. But wouldn't everyone be glad to see him? Speculating gave him little comfort. The sun was still directly overhead. It seemed to Charlie he had been studying his options for at least an hour or more yet the sun had stayed in the same position. He guessed his estimate of time was off. He'd take a walk. There had to be a way out.

The sand warmed his feet as he strolled toward the end of the beach where the promontory of rocks cascaded into the ocean. He searched the rocky formation for anything that would allow him to go through. The tide was just beginning to recede pulling its frothy wake back into the ocean. It was then that he saw it . . . a small opening nestled between two large rocks. The onshore waves covered it until the tide took its leave. He quickly stepped through. Before him lay what looked to be a mile long beach. It was deserted except for a small group of men huddled around a rubber raft about fifty feet away. It looked like the men had been diving. Their equipment was scattered around the raft. Charlie heard one of them yell to another.

"We found him, but too late. Bring the stretcher." Charlie ran closer to see . . . then he heard someone say, "Poor kid. What was his name? Charlie? Notify the Whitfields right away. How long has he been missing? Three days?"

Charlie stood stone still unable to grasp the meaning of what he had just seen and heard. Stunned, he slowly sank to his knees. At that moment, a hand touched him. Its warmth filled him lifting him up covering him in golden radiant light so intricate, so full of love, that he could hardly contain it. A tremendous sense of peace, joy, and belonging filled his heart. A soft voice whispered, *You're home now, Charlie.* And he knew he was.

Two Weeks

❖

So do not fear, for I am with you,
Do not be dismayed, for I am your God
I will strengthen you and help you.
- Isaiah 41:19

Jan knew this day would change her life forever. How long had she waited, prayed, and hoped? She had come a long way and now the door stood ajar. Which way would it swing? Open or closed?

The last seven years of her life were ones she did not ask for, nor would she have given them away to anyone. She alone had to own them—each and every one vividly inscribed in her mind—years of treatment as she suffered the fierce side effects of radiation. Chemo had been a walk in the park compared to the retching and exhaustion from radiation.

"The Death March of the Body." "The Killing Fields." These were her terms for it. Then came the experimental drugs. With each injection placed expertly into the port that had been surgically implanted in her chest, came hope and the promise that each new drug would bring her back, present the cure that she had desperately prayed for. Had she not lost part of herself and a loss of hope with each new drug?

It was her choice of course. The oncologist did not force her, but how could she refuse a chance for hope? Wasn't it worth going through the side effects, the pain, the loss of her beautiful thick long hair? It was worth it. Wasn't it?

She sat quietly waiting for the doctor, the four walls pushing into her, compressing her ability to breathe. In her heart she prayed there would still be one more drug that would bring her back—that would take away all of those lost years of suffering. Seven years. Had she not qualified for some sort of award, a prize perhaps for being willing to try and then try again? No matter what the cost, she was a hero, but the cost had turned out to be way over the top expensive.

Tomorrow was her birthday. Forty-six. She was still willing to go for it. 'One more time please, I am not ready to die. I still have a life to live,' she said to herself.

The door opened. The oncologist entered the room quietly, not smiling, his face a somber mask. A tremor shot down her spine. She didn't want to hear. Her heart began to pound in her ears. She prayed the pulsing sound would shut out the words that he was about to speak, the words that would eliminate her existence. She perceived his words as mouthed and read his lips because her ears refused to listen.

"Prepare yourself, Jan. I am so sorry to have to bring bad news, but you must be strong, courageous." What did he think she had been doing for seven years?

She had been strong and courageous, and now he was asking for more? She had no more to give.

"There is nothing left to be done." He took her hand. "You must contact Hospice. They will help you, take care of you, and be there for you 24/7."

"How long doctor?"

He looked directly into her eyes that were brimming with tears. "Two, maybe three weeks. You must tell your family."

"I have no family."

He gave her hand a squeeze. "If you have questions, Jan, please call. A nurse will be in shortly to help you get started with Hospice."

The tears would not stop. They became uncontrolled sobs. Her cry for help had not been answered. Her body wrenched in pain, heartsick pain. Finally her tears gave way to agony. The deep pain of denial ripped apart her resolve, her strength, leaving only shreds of what was once her. She was left without purpose, a walking corpse. What had the seven years of hope been for?

Just then an epiphany struck her. It rushed into her head as if it were alive, shaking her. The thought rose to a screaming crescendo. Were these tears of relief? Could that possibly be? Was she not now relieved of this heavy burden that had driven her life for so long? Why had she crumbled in fear? Clarity spanned her vision. Suddenly she had a realization so endearing, so close . . . and knew she had nothing to fear. The Lord was with her; he had been with her through it all. All of the hope, pain, and defeat, and even now, the last defeat. It sat in the room nudging her. But it would not overtake her. It wouldn't win. Isaiah 41:4 resounded loudly within her spirit.

"Do not fear for I am with you. Do not be dismayed for I am your God. I will strengthen you and help you." She realized that she had just spent her strength in vain, through tears of fear and remorse, for nothing. For the Lord's hand was upon her. She instinctively knew this, and that his strength would carry her. A peace that defies understanding welled up inside of her.

She wiped the tears from her eyes just as the Hospice nurse opened the door.

A Beach Day:
Big Island Hawaii

❧

I can hardly wait to get there. I drive alone on the
curving mountain road that leads toward the sea. My spirit
yearns for the beauty of the ocean.

One more turn and there it is—that clear turquoise
which infuses perfect serenity. Exiting off the highway
onto the dirt road saying "Beach Access," I park near a
clump of ki'awe trees and walk carefully toward the beach,
being watchful not to step on the thorns that are native to
these trees. They lie in wait for those not familiar with the
natural terrain.

Finally reaching the beach, I kick off my flip-flops.
The early morning warmth and softness of white sand
spills between my toes. I dig my toes deeper into the
depth of the sand; a coolness lingers there from the night
tide. The sensation is comforting, cozy.

There is a nice, shady place behind an outcropping
of lava rocks just ahead. *I hope no one has claimed it.* It is
secluded and sheltered, mirroring a small private cove.
Dragging the beach chair and my bag the ten feet or so it
takes to get there is challenging, but the reward is worth it.
With no one around, I can relax in the shade of the
Ironwood tree that lives here. I set up my chair and place
the ice carrier containing a drink and a papaya next to the
tree trunk.

The morning sun is hot and the waves seem to be flat, so I'm encouraged to swim now rather than wait until later when the wind kicks up. Walking toward the white froth that laps onto the beach and standing in its foamy wake renews my energy and my spirit, as the sun's heat penetrates my body. The lazy motion of the oncoming waves brush lightly against my legs as I wade in and dive under. The water is languid and crystal clear. The sandy bottom comes up to meet my gaze. I view sudden flashes of striking colors; orange, blue, and yellow worn by tropical fish that adorn the coral reef. I stroke out beyond the breakers. Stopping a little way out, I turn onto my back and float. The motion of the water is invigorating as it laps against my body.

I drink in the sky above. It is a never-ending vastness of blue. My muscles start letting go and the tension releases as relaxation ebbs its way into my soul. Agility and a lightness of being fill me. Just when I'm thinking, *Is there anything better?* I feel something rough underneath me. *There are no rocks, so what could it be?* I almost freeze as the thought of 'shark bait' pierces my mind when suddenly, to my great relief, the head of a gigantic sea turtle surfaces a mere arm's length away. The dip and sway of its shell moves gracefully, as its flippers paddle in a circle around me creating an aquatic ballet. I wonder if the turtle is inviting me to swim. I try to touch its head, but it ducks and starts to swim away.

No, not yet. I want to spend more time with you. Swimming forward, I catch up with this beautiful sea creature. Now, we swim side by side. What a thrill. I notice it eyeing me several times. *Could it be frightened?* I don't want to frighten it so I hold back a little just to make sure. As I do the turtle dives under. I decide to follow but without goggles I can only stay under a short while before the salt water begins to sting my eyes. I can see it just ahead of me but my vision becomes blurry and I must surface. I don't want to lose sight of my turtle so I dive once more and catch a glimpse as it ascends to the surface. It turns suddenly, swimming toward shore. I follow. It swims to a hidden patch of beach, crawls onto shore and nestles itself into a deep sandy spot next to a lava rock tide pool.

My newfound friend's eyes investigate me as I slowly sit down. *Not too close—just close enough to let it know I'm here.* Watching, I observe its peaceful state. Its eyes become heavy and slowly close. I, too, relax, confident that it trusts me.

Sitting next to my turtle and absorbing the sun, I observe several more sea turtles climbing onto the shore. My presence does not seem to disturb them as they head for their sandy spots. The warmth of the sand must soothe their bellies and with the sun beating upon their shells they are lulled into deep sleep.

Viewing the beauty that surrounds me my mind creates a vision for a lasting image. The white sandy beach, enclosed by rocky masses formed by ancient lava flows, nurtures succulent plants, which push through the porous black surface. Tide pools jut outward capturing the flow of wave activity, entrapping the water, and providing a safe haven for many species of embryonic fish. Reds, yellows . . . even the small tadpoles have a bluish tint to their transparent forms. The pools become a tropical aquarium, lasting only for a second before the rush of waves spill into them, then quickly pull out to make way for the next rush. A continuing ritual by Mother Nature to preserve her young.

Long shadows have begun to trace images in the sand. The afternoon has flown. I cannot tear myself away from the nearness of my turtle friend, even though the lackadaisical motion of the surf creeps closer with each return . . . the tide reclaiming its evening vigil. Reaching out, I touch the hard shell of my turtle as a gesture of friendship. The warmth of its shell surprises me. I let my hand linger. *Thank you, my friend, for sharing your peace. You showed me how to let go of anxiety and stress.*

I move back to the rock formation behind me and find a flat dry surface to rest upon. My turtle stays put; he is safely perched on his rocky plateau. The sun is now low on the horizon. It has a clean descent into the sea, which means, if I look carefully, there will be a green flash just before it deposits itself behind the rim of the earth. I do not move my gaze and there, in the blink of an eye is the flash. It stays with me long after the sun has disappeared. Ribbons of gold, orange, blue and pink parade across the evening sky resembling an intricate paradigm. Lingering splashes of vibrant reds finally give way to an orange glow that remains even after the first star appears.

I walk slowly along the shore heading back to the Ironwood tree to gather my belongings. The sand is cool under my feet, but the horizon's glow warms me as I drink in the orange-red aftertaste of the sunset.

Driving back up the hill I reminisce about my life on the Big Island of Hawaii. When I first moved here it was to embrace my family. Over the years I have found a refuge, an environment that pours itself over me like cleansing rain. Of course, there are the everyday routines and concerns, but all I have to do is take a walk in the rain forest, or view the orchid plants that adorn my porch, or best of all, go down to the beach and look for my honu (turtle) friend to thank him for awakening in me a new sense of self by inviting me into his world. I wonder even now if he still lingers peacefully in the warmth of his sandy oasis on that hidden beach.

Acknowledgments

❧

I thank my wife, Cecilia Branch, for her birthday gift of a seven-week creative writing class at the Walnut Creek Adult Center that was the beginning of the odyssey culminating in this anthology.

I further thank Janice De Jesus, who has been my creative writing instructor (and later, editor) from 2013 to the present. She has become a friend and the wellspring of all my creative writing endeavors.

I am indebted to Charlie Burke (aka Carlos) for inviting me to participate in the anthology group in March 2014, enabling me to share my writing with all the other members of our writing group.

Finally, I thank Karen Mireau at Azalea Art Press for her patience, insight, capabilities and skills in bringing our writers' efforts to publication.

- Ken Branch

I wish to thank the staff at Grace Healthcare, especially Sharon Lobato, the Activities Director, for encouraging me to keep active in my writing.

I also want to thank Janice De Jesus for challenging me to enhance my writing skills and introducing me to this talented writer's group, who have accepted me as a peer into their association.

Finally, my gratitude to Karen Mireau for being the Maestro organizer; and last, but not least, to Barbara Burgess for supporting my writing for the last thirty-five years.

- Douglas Burgess

Congratulations to the authors included in this anthology. They have worked hard to compile an exciting series of stories that will produce tremors in and among the readers.

Special thanks go to Janice De Jesus and Karen Mireau for their support, advice and guidance throughout the writing-publishing process. Both Janice and Karen continue to be inspirations.

- Franklin T. Burroughs

Manjari and the Ballad of Peace is dedicated to my mother, the late Mrs. Biva Mitra.

Many thanks to Mr. Amitabha Basu for the translation of Rabindra Nath Tagore's song *Jadi tor dak shune kau na ashe tobe ekla cholo re* from Bengalee to English.

- Maya Mitra Das

My association with the other seven contributors to *Tremors* will stay with me forever.

To my family back east who supported my efforts in this project from the beginning and can't wait to see the finished product.

To Lynne Westenhaver who took charge and herded us eight cats to the finish line with a publication we can all relish. To Ana, Ceci, and Maura, in the Wednesday writing group, for some great critiquing and for advising me every week not to quit my day job. They have heard my stories often enough to have them memorized.

To Lyn Roberts, my editor, who pushed me and corrected my stories for bad content and other miscues to make them acceptable for public consumption. To Karen Mireau, who distilled more than 70 stories down to the 27

290

in our anthology. Karen made a daunting task look easy.

And to our creativity guru, Janice De Jesus, who made us all better writers and who conceived the idea of the anthology two years ago. Janice, you're my soul and my highest inspiration!

- Carlos de Jalisco

First, I thank Janice De Jesus, whose creative writing course pulled me back into fiction writing in 2010. She is dedicated to sharing with her students the wonders of exploring the world through their own words.

Next, our team of authors, who have spent many hours listening to one another's writing and offering constructive comments—thanks for taking on the thorny job of final edits for some of my stories and for the valuable feedback.

I want to acknowledge my writing roots: Bob Salem, English teacher in junior and senior years of high school, supported my efforts wholeheartedly and was an inspiration to continue writing. Currently, my friend Karolyn Dreyer, who produced "The Twinkle Stars" with me in 2010, is one of my main supporters.

To my husband Jeff Bell and my family of origin, who said, "You can do it" whenever I have voiced doubts, my heart-felt thanks.

- Sue Hummel

To the people in my life who have touched me and left an indelible mark on my heart and soul; I thank you. You have shaped who I am, and so you live among the pages of my stories.

With deep love and gratitude, I dedicate this book to the remembrance of those who have died; to William and Cecilia, my parents; to Clarissa and Elizabeth, my sisters; and to my husband Jim. To my adult children, Stanley, Katherine, Elizabeth, and Sarah, three son-in-laws, Chano, Curt and Joel, and five grandchildren, Zachary, Cody, Ashlyn, Mateo, and Landon—who taught me to love—I thank you.

To Janice De Jesus, Creative Writing Instructor, my thanks for her nurturing and positive teaching style, one that inspired and challenged me to excel. To Lyn Roberts, my editor, I am indebted for her corrections, enthusiasm and gentle insistence for "more," which helped me to polish my stories.

For the critiques and support of my writing family and friends who walked this journey with me, and to Karen Mireau of Azalea Press, whose expertise will immortalize our words between the covers of this book; I am forever grateful.

- Cecilia Pugh

To all of the authors who comprise this body of work, I want to say thanks: thanks for your creativity, your determination, your taking that next step and standing strong. Thank you for those times when the odds were not favorable you ignored them and moved forward. The first step is the beginning and we have begun . . . hats off to you.

To Janice De Jesus, you are our inspiration. We thank you for bringing us together and teaching us how to dance with words.

To our Publisher Karen Mireau—where would we have gone if not for you? You gathered us and put us in order. Then you gently and creatively set the direction and established the process.

To Sharon Stewart—your remarkable input, edits and hand holding kept me together. Thanks to you, my friend. Thanks also for other edits from Lyn Roberts that are very much appreciated.

To my family and my close friends who are also my family, I thank you for your enthusiastic response. Your encouragement and support sustained me.

- Lynne Grant-Westenhaver

Book Orders:
www.lulu.com

Azalea Art Press
azaleaartpress@gmail.com

Karen Mireau
Publisher / Literary Midwife

Visit:
http://tremorsanthology.blogspot.com